ROCK GUITAR SOLOING

ADVANCED PROFESSIONAL TECHNIQUES

THEORY & HARMONY • UNUSUAL METERS & RHYTHMS • EXOTIC SCALES • MODERN BLUES • 120 AUDIO EXAMPLES

Pablo Pescatore

To access the online audio, go to:
WWW.MELBAY.COM/30943MEB

WWW.MELBAY.COM

Table of Contents

Acknowledgements

To my wife, Maria de los Angeles Galli and my children: Sofia, Lucia and Vitto.

To my mother and my entire family.

To Mr. William Bay and his editorial team at Mel Bay Publications for trusting in my work.

To music and text editor, Stephen Rekas—for always encouraging me with his knowledge and wisdom.

Thank you!

To all my students and friends, including Osman López and Greisy Pérez at the Arpeggio Music Academy, Julio Rocella and Santiago Calcagno of *MX Magazine*, my former student and always friend—Sebastián Bustamente.

To Arturo Mawcinitt and Seymour Duncan, developer and manufacturer of my SH-8 Invader pickups. To Skull Strings for their sponsorship, recording technician, Luciano Altamirano, and to all those who accompany me on this musical journey—I cannot overstate my gratitude to you all.

IN MEMORY OF MY FATHER

PEDRO PESCATORE (1948-2015)

Preface

Once upon a time in America, you could get a job teaching rock guitar in a music shop if you could play the introductory riff to the latest hit tune. Nowadays, to the credit of institutions of higher learning and music shop owners throughout the country, that is no longer the case. It is now possible to declare a major in jazz or classical guitar performance at many American colleges and universities, and you may have to present some credentials to get that music shop teaching gig. It is now up to those college graduates to bring hobbyist and beginning guitarists up to par in their knowledge of music theory and standard notation sightreading ability, at last fulfilling the vision that Mel Bay had in writing his *Modern Guitar Method.*

I got to know Pablo Pescatore while editing *Complete Guide to Shred Guitar*, his first book for Mel Bay Publications. From the first track, my jaw dropped when I heard the speed of the slower, *student* audio examples, let alone the pedal-to-the-metal performance speed. It was immediately evident that we were dealing with an exceptionally well-educated musician and an amazing guitarist.

While inspired by many of the same guitar heroes as his North American counterparts, Pablo took his music education seriously and graduated with honors from a school for development of professional musicians in Buenos Aires, Argentina. In the process, he became a virtuoso electric and classic guitarist, fluid in several styles but specializing in rock. Pablo not only has a great ear for rock guitar licks and technique; he is well-schooled as a composer, music theorist and teacher of sight singing.

If you are an acoustic guitarist who does not yet own an electric guitar, you'll want to get one after hearing the tracks recorded for this book. Without seeing the manuscript or hearing the first track of *Extreme Rock Guitar Soloing*, I knew that Pablo's second book would be rich in content, the music would be properly written, and the audio tracks would be brilliantly played with attention to tone, dynamics and tempo; in other words, not just fast, clean and loud.

Extreme Rock Guitar Soloing presents a masterclass in applied music theory. Pablo lays out the theory principles and then demonstrates them in 120 recorded examples featuring guitar, drumset and organ. Throughout, he encourages readers to write similar phrases in standard notation and incorporate them in their own solos.

Consider the following: At whatever level you have attained as a guitarist, it is virtually impossible for you to write anything you can't play. If you accept Pablo's invitation to accompany him on this musical journey, you will not only have an original body of work to draw from in your soloing, but—because you have written it on paper instead of "in your head"— you will also have become a much better sight reader. This asset alone will open many doors for you. If you truly want to become a better rock and blues guitar soloist, indeed, a better musician—you are holding the key in your hands.

For Mel Bay Publications,
Stephen B. Rekas
Music & Text Editor

CHAPTER 1

Melodic and Harmonic Aspects of Rock Guitar Soloing

Introduction

Welcome to my take on the art and craft of rock guitar soloing. I have called this book *Extreme Rock Guitar Soloing* because I intend to explore this topic to its limits and beyond. I hope it will expand not only your possible *choices* and creativity as a rock guitar soloist, but also augment your awareness of music theory and musicianship in general. Contrary to the advice of various internet guitar gurus, you will have to practice scales, a lot of them- but I promise that you will benefit from it. Finally, to get the most from this book and become a better sight reader, keep a record of your ideas in standard notation.

Before we begin, here are some essential theoretical concepts to keep in mind:

scale — A succession of tones arranged in a set pattern. Twelve sounds are used in our musical system, seven being natural **(C, D, E, F, G, A, B),** and five being altered **(C♯/D♭, D♯/E♭, F♯/G♭, G♯//A♭, A♯//B♭).**
adjacent grades— Degrees of the scale that are next to one another, for example: C-D.
non-adjacent grades— Scale tones that are not next to each other, for example: C-G.
whole tone— The greatest distance between two adjoining diatonic scale degrees, represented as **W.**
half tone— The shortest distance between two adjoining diatonic scale degrees, represented as **H.**
interval— The distance between two musical tones, measured according to the degrees that they comprise. For example: C-D (major second), C-E (major third), C-F (perfect fourth), etc.
chord— Traditionally, three or more tones sounded together.
tetrachord— Not actually a chord, but rather one of a pair of four adjoining scale tones separated by a whole step into **lower** and **upper** tetrachords.

More terminology and definitions will be added as needed.

The following table illustrates the intervals between the fundamental or tonic (I) and the other degrees of a C chromatic scale.

Interval Table

STEPS	INTERVAL	EXAMPLE FROM C
0 Steps	Perfect Unison	C to C
1/2 Step	Minor 2nd	C to C♯/D♭
1 Whole Step	Major 2nd	C to D
1 and 1/2 Steps	Minor 3rd	C to D♯/E♭
2 Whole Steps	Major 3rd	C to E
2 and 1/2 Steps	Perfect 4th	C to F
3 Whole Steps	Augmented 4th	C to F♯/G♭
3 and 1/2 Steps	Perfect 5th	C to G
4 Whole Steps	Aug. 5th/Minor 6th	C to G♯/A♭
4 and 1/2 Steps	Major 6th	C to A
5 Whole Steps	Minor 7th/Aug. 6th	C to A♯/B♭
5 and 1/2 Steps	Major 7th	C to B
6 Whole Steps	Perfect Octave	C to C

THE MAJOR SCALE

The major scale, derived from the Ionian mode, is the basis of our musical system. It is made up of five whole-steps (W) and two half-steps (H)— the natural half tones, E-F and B-C— grouped in a certain order and criterion **(WWHWWWH)**, establishing a consistent intervallic structure for all major scales. It is composed of two identical major **tetrachords**, a succession of four adjoining scale tones separated by a whole step. The first tetrachord formed by the lower notes is called the **lower tetrachord**, while the second formed by the higher notes is called the **upper tetrachord**.

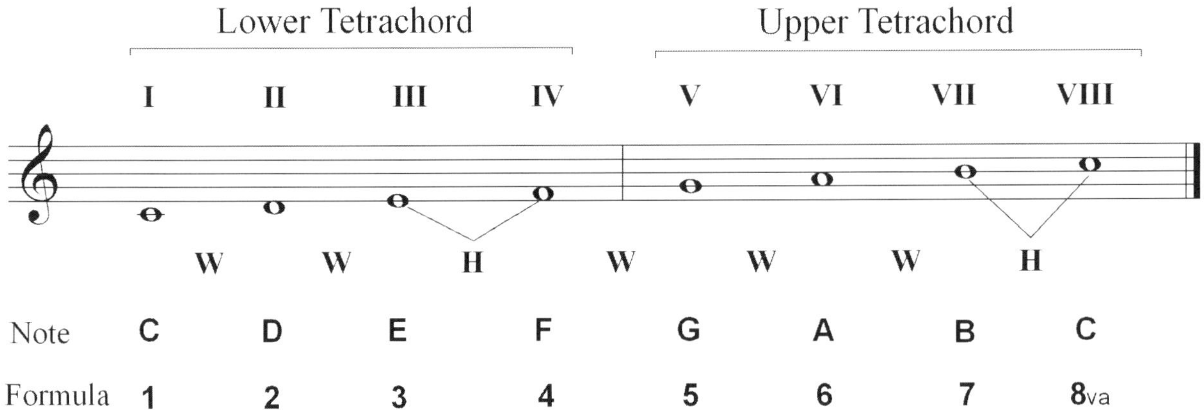

If we take the upper tetrachord of the C major scale and turn it into a lower tetrachord, we get the G major scale; to complete the notes of the upper tetrachord we only need to assign a sharp to the seventh degree (F♯) to preserve the structure of the C major **model scale**. Repeating this procedure will yield all the major scales with sharps, ultimately creating the **Circle of Fifths:** G – D – A – E – B – F♯ where G has one sharp, D has two sharps, etc.
(See Example 1).
In the case of scales with flats, the procedure consists of taking the lower tetrachord of the C major scale and making it the upper tetrachord of the F major scale. To complete this lower tetrachord, we only need to add a flat to the fourth degree of the scale, B**.** Continuing in this manner, we can construct all of the flat-bearing major scales, this time revealing the **Circle of Fourths:** F – B♭ – E♭ – A♭ – D♭ – G♭ where F has one flat, B♭ has two flats, etc.
(See Example 2).

Example 1

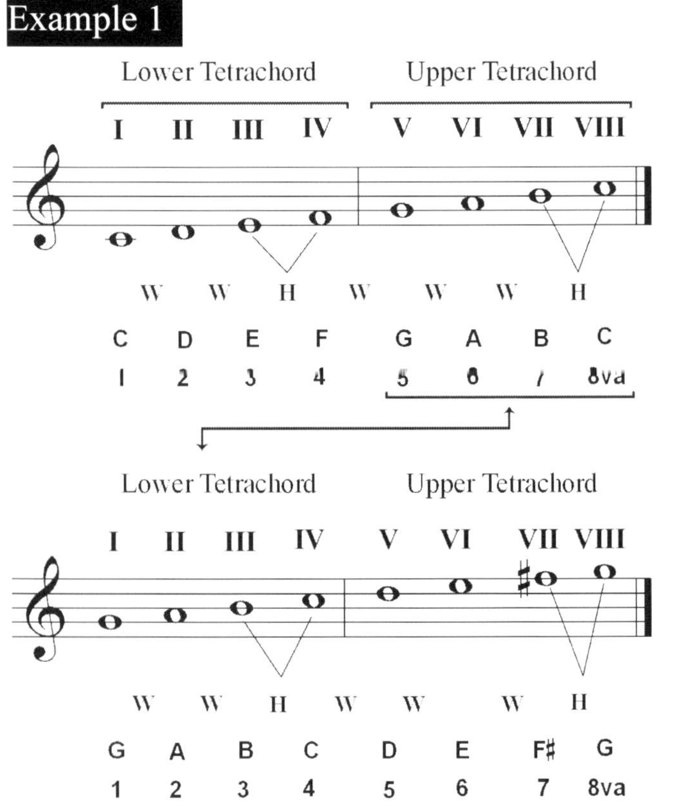

Example 2

Traditionally, each tone generated in the scale is identified by means of a Roman numeral assigned according to its location; the modern system uses common Arabic numbers, as in the Nashville Numbering System.

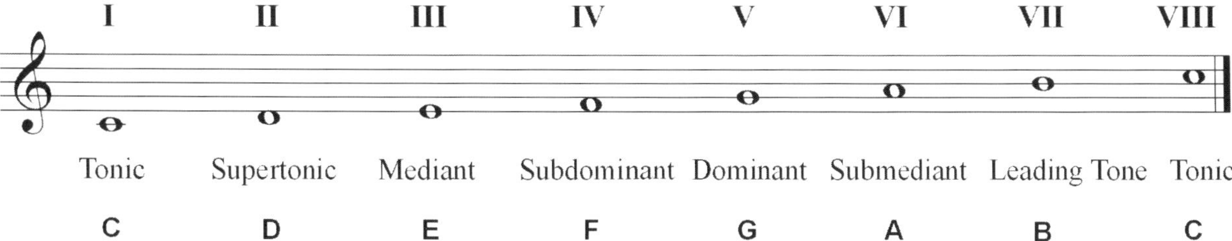

Tonic	Supertonic	Mediant	Subdominant	Dominant	Submediant	Leading Tone	Tonic
C	D	E	F	G	A	B	C

Note that in major scales, degrees VII and VIII are only a half tone apart and the "leading tone" tendency back to the tonic is very strong. In the pure minor scale, the VII and VIII degrees are separated by a whole tone and there is less of a "leading" towards the tonic. For this reason, the 7th degree of the pure or natural minor scale is often referred to as the **subtonic**.

Example 3

Track 1

In our first recorded example we play an ascending and descending pattern based on the C major scale. **Play this exercise in all major keys.** As all the notes are "stopped" or fretted, this is not so great a task as it may seem at first. Using a pencil, so you can change your mind—add left-hand fingering as needed.

TAB

8–10–12–8–10–12–8–10 | 12–8–10–12–8–10–12–8 | 10–12–9–10–12–9–10–12 | 9–10–12–9–10

5

10–12–9–10–12–9–10–12 | 9–10–12–9–10–12–10–10 | 12–10–12–12–10–12–13–10 | 12–13–10–12–13

9

13–12–10–13–12–10–12–12 | 10–12–10–10–12–10–9–12 | 10–9–12–10–9–12–10–9 | 12–10–9–12–10

13

10–9–12–10–9–12–10–9 | 12–10–8–12–10–8–12–10 | 8–12–10–8–12–10–8–12 | 10–8–7–10–8

THE NATURAL MINOR SCALE

The natural or pure minor scale is derived from the sixth degree of its relative major scale. This scale has lowered degrees 3, 6 and 7 with respect to the tonic and in relation to the major scale. It is made up of a minor tetrachord and a Phrygian tetrachord.

Note that the main characteristic that differentiates the pure minor scale from the major scale is that the third degree is 1 and 1/2 steps—a minor third—from the tonic. Both scales are made up of the same notes but with a different tonal center or tonic note.

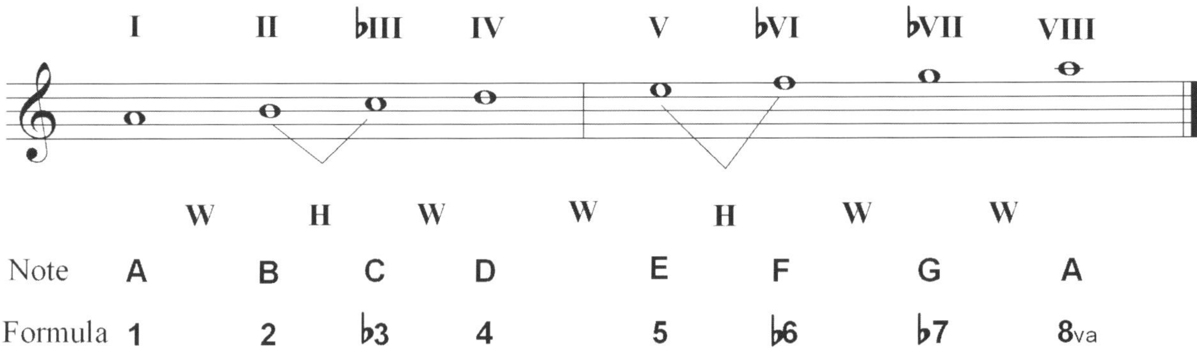

Example 4 **Track 2**

In the following phrase, we use the natural minor scale over a typical minor key progression.

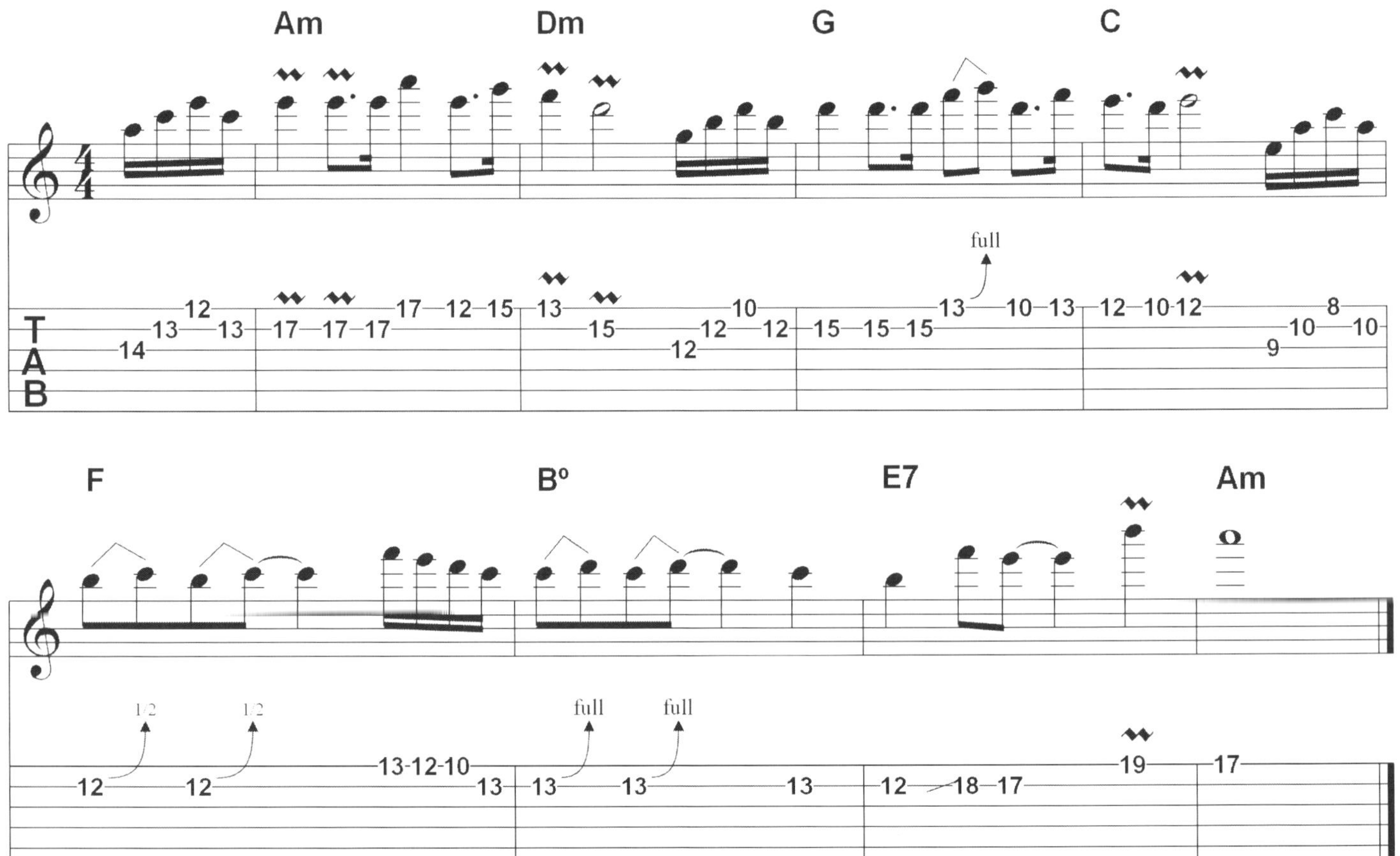

THE HARMONIC MINOR SCALE

When studying the natural or pure minor scale we observed that its seventh degree is a whole step away from the tonic; this causes the scale to lack a leading tone and consequently it does not generate a resolution towards the tonic. To correct this issue, it was decided to raise the seventh degree of the natural minor scale by a half step, giving rise to the **harmonic minor scale**. In addition, this alteration achieved the formation of a dominant seventh chord on its fifth degree, solving the harmonic problem presented by the natural minor scale, hence the name of this scale. With respect to the major scale, the harmonic minor scale has lowered 3rd and 6th degrees. This scale is formed by a minor tetrachord followed by a harmonic tetrachord.

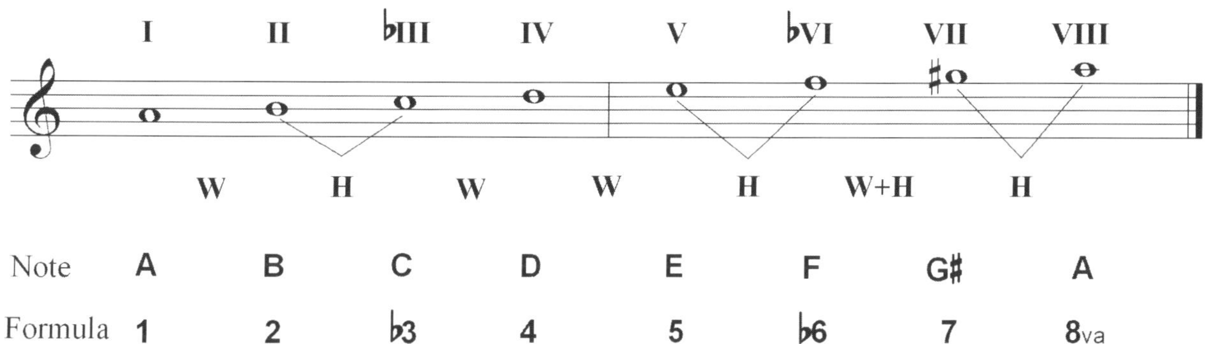

Example 5

Track 3

The following example illustrates the application of the harmonic minor scale over an Am progression. **Pay close attention to the chord changes and the use of the harmonic minor scale over them.**

THE MELODIC MINOR SCALE

The leap of the augmented second **(♯2)** between the sixth and seventh degrees of the harmonic minor scale is an unnatural interval to our ears. To correct this inconvenience and favor the melodic passage between said degrees, it was decided to raise the sixth degree by a half tone: **A-B-C-D-E-F♯-G♯-A**. The melodic minor scale is then built by raising the 6th and 7th degrees of the natural minor scale on the ascent only. To preserve the minor sonority, this scale descends by suppressing those two accidentals; since this scale has a minor tetrachord followed by a major one, the only note that differs from the major scale is its minor third. To obtain an ascending melodic minor scale, all we need to do is lower the third degree of the major scale by a half tone.

Since both the harmonic minor and melodic minor scales have been modified by means of accidentals, they are regarded as *artificial scales*; consequently, they do not have their own representative key signatures.

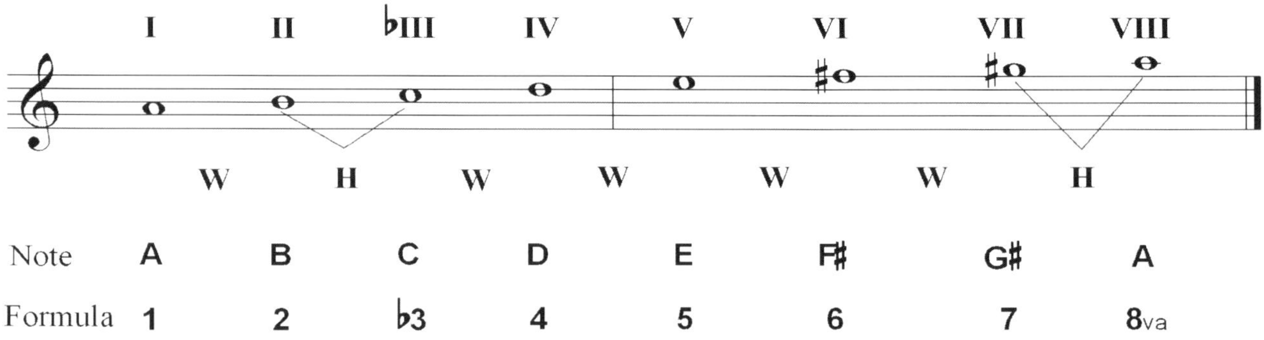

Note	A	B	C	D	E	F♯	G♯	A
Formula	1	2	♭3	4	5	6	7	8va

Example 6 **Track 4**

In the following example we start by playing the melodic minor scale in the first two measures **(A-B-C-D-E-F♯-G♯-A)** and descend with the natural minor scale in measures 3 and 4 **(A-G-F-E-D-C-B-A)**.

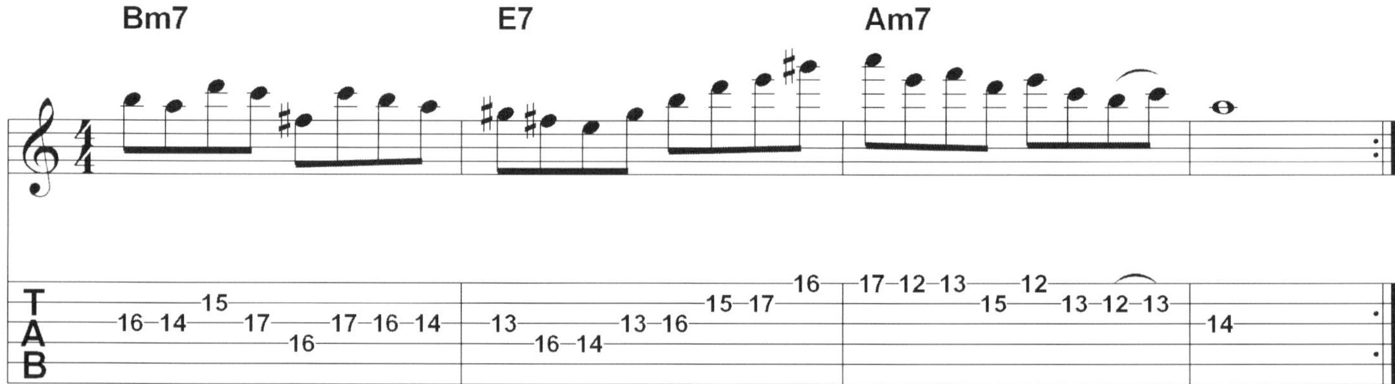

MODAL SCALES

Each degree of a major scale can serve as the tonic or starting point for a new scale. These scales were called **modes** by church musicians during the Middle Ages and were given classical Greek names:

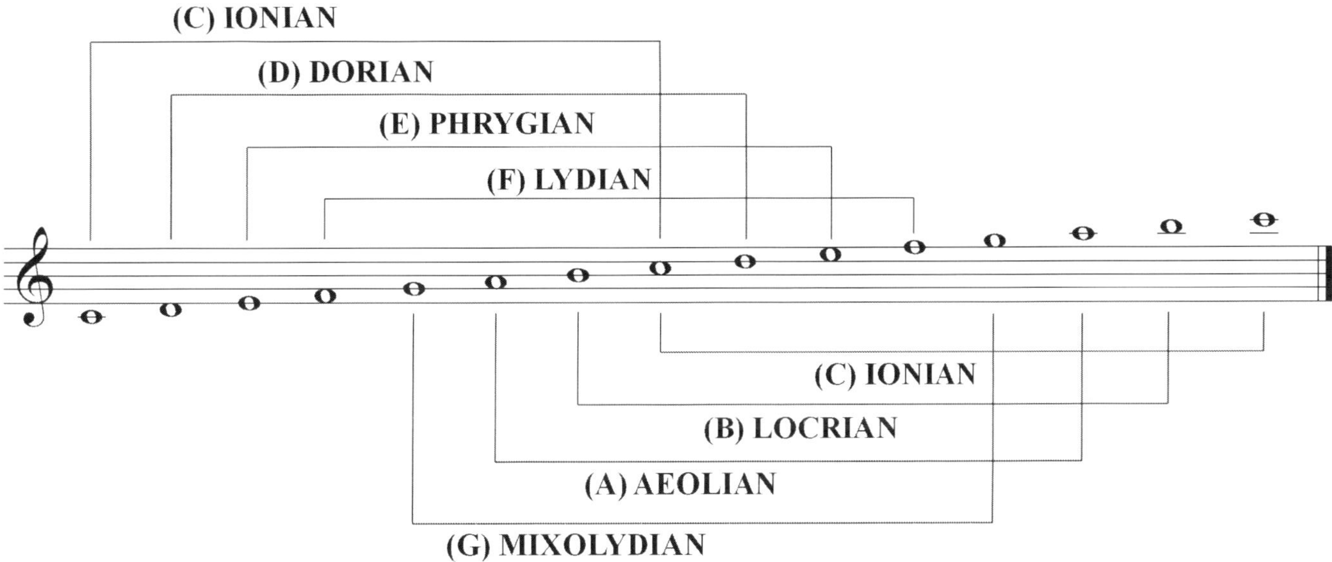

There are seven modes corresponding to the seven distinctive tones of the major scale.

1. THE IONIAN MODE

The Ionian mode is formed by two major tetrachords; its formula is: 1-2-3-4-5-6-7. We know it simply as the *major* scale.

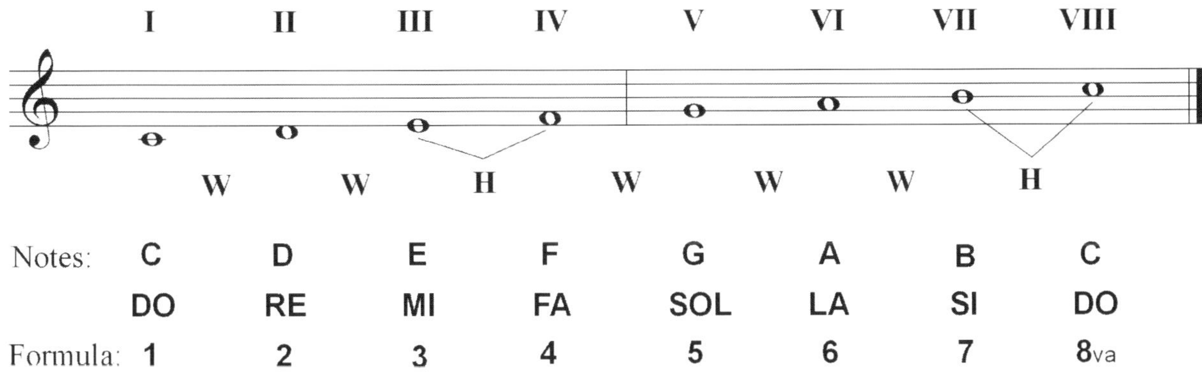

To learn the sound and *feel* of the seven modal scales, it´s a good idea to sing them in solfege syllables while playing them on the guitar or piano.

2. THE DORIAN MODE:

This mode is made up of two minor tetrachords with flatted third and seventh degrees.
Its formula is: 1-2-♭3-4-5-6-♭7.

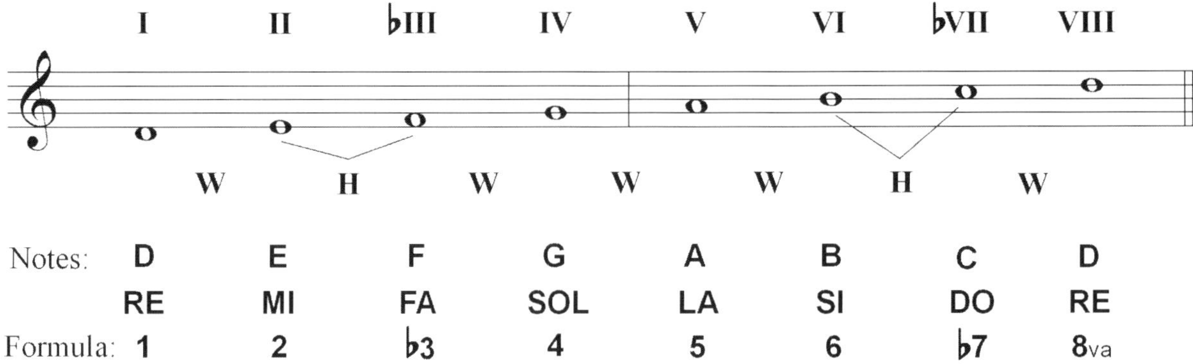

3. THE PHRYGIAN MODE

This mode is made up of two Phrygian tetrachords; it contains minor second, minor third, minor sixth and minor seventh intervals. Its formula is: 1-♭2-♭3-4-5-♭6-♭7.

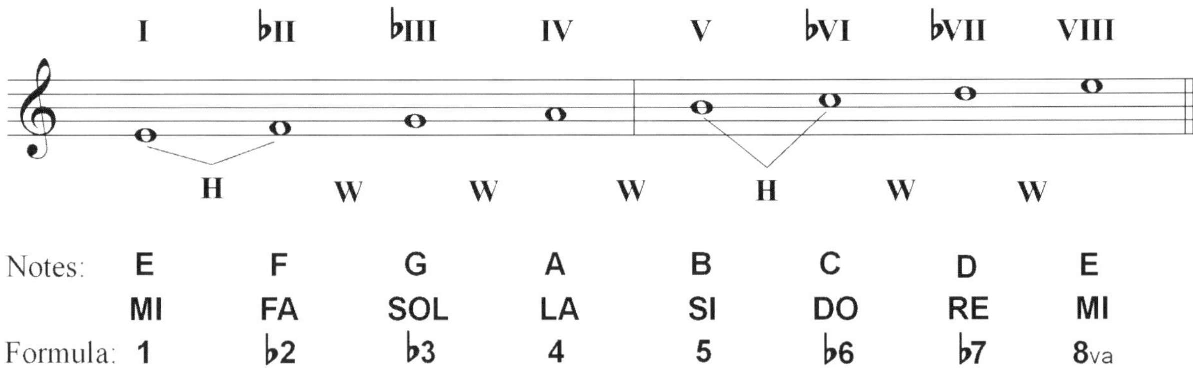

4. THE LYDIAN MODE

This mode is formed by an augmented tetrachord followed by a major tetrachord; it contains the augmented fourth. Its formula is: 1-2-3-♯4-5-6-7.

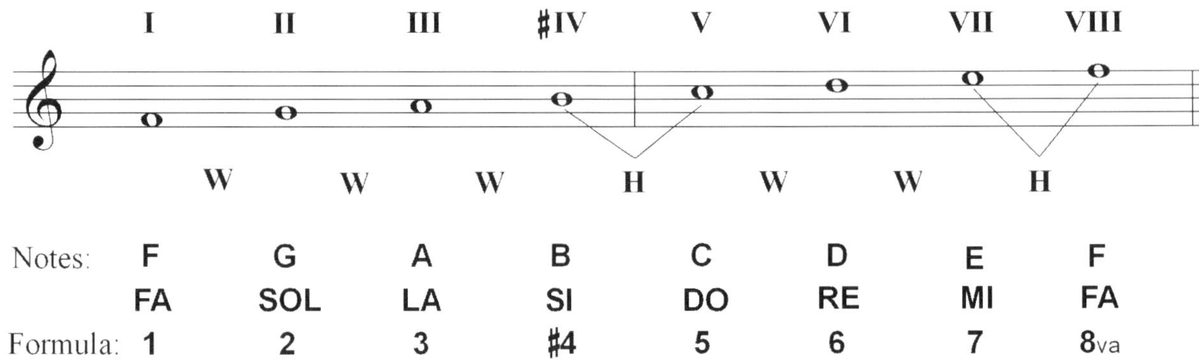

5. THE MIXOLYDIAN MODE

This mode is formed by a major tetrachord followed by a minor tetrachord containing a minor seventh interval. The formula for the Mixolydian modal scale is: 1-2-3-4-5-6-♭7.

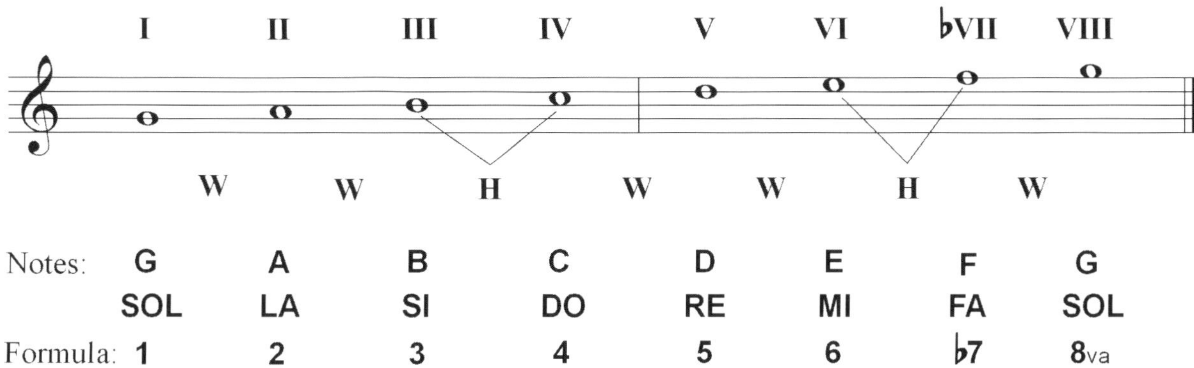

6. THE AEOLIAN MODE

This mode is formed by a minor tetrachord followed by a Phrygian tetrachord, and contains minor third, sixth and seventh intervals. Its formula is: 1-2-♭3-4-5-♭6-♭7. We know it as the *natural* or *pure minor* scale.

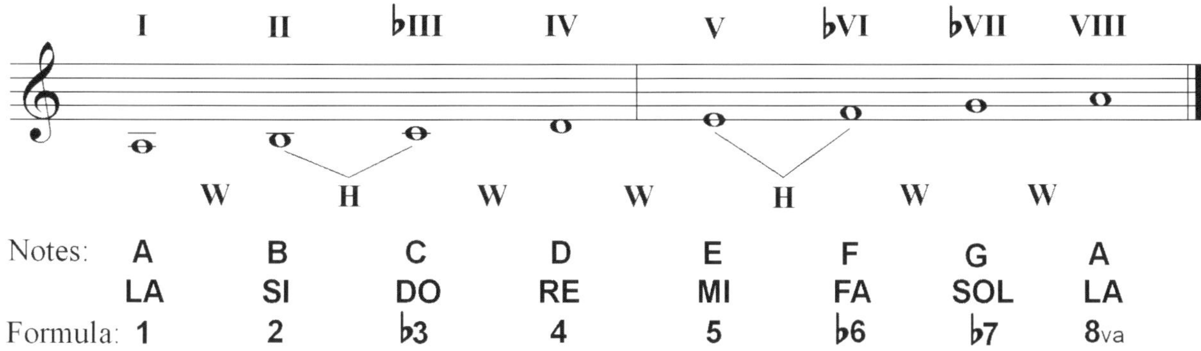

7. THE LOCRIAN MODE

The Locrian mode is formed by a Phrygian tetrachord followed by an augmented tetrachord; it contains the minor second, minor third, diminished fifth, minor sixth and minor seventh intervals.
Its formula is: 1-♭2-♭3-4-♭5-♭6-♭7.

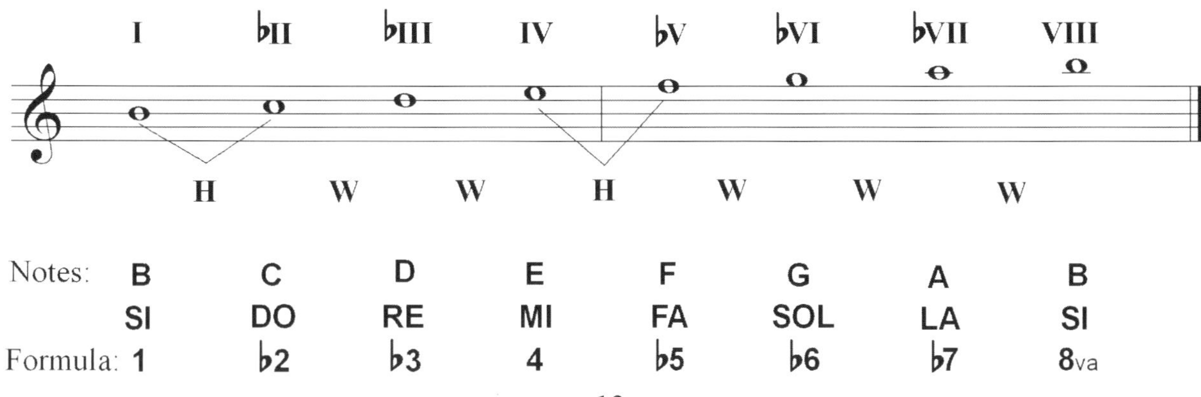

Each mode has its own structure and sonority that makes it easily recognizable.

IONIAN	Luminous major scale
DORIAN	Minor sonority, soft fusion-style
PHRYGIAN	Dark, flamenco-style sound
LYDIAN	Enigmatic, mystical sonority
MIXOLYDIAN	Bluesy sound
AEOLIAN	Sad, melancholic pure minor sonority
LOCRIAN	Gloomy and unstable

These sensations are subjective, of course; the idea is to be able to understand how modes convey different states of mind and how they influence music.

It is very important to memorize the name, sound and feel of each mode.

Example 7

Track 5

In the following example we play each of the modes on the respective chords in the key of C major.

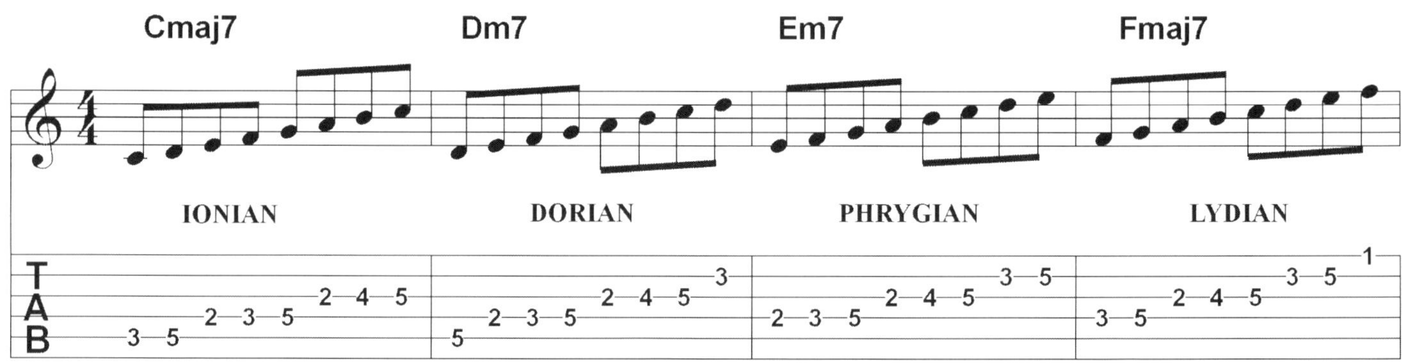

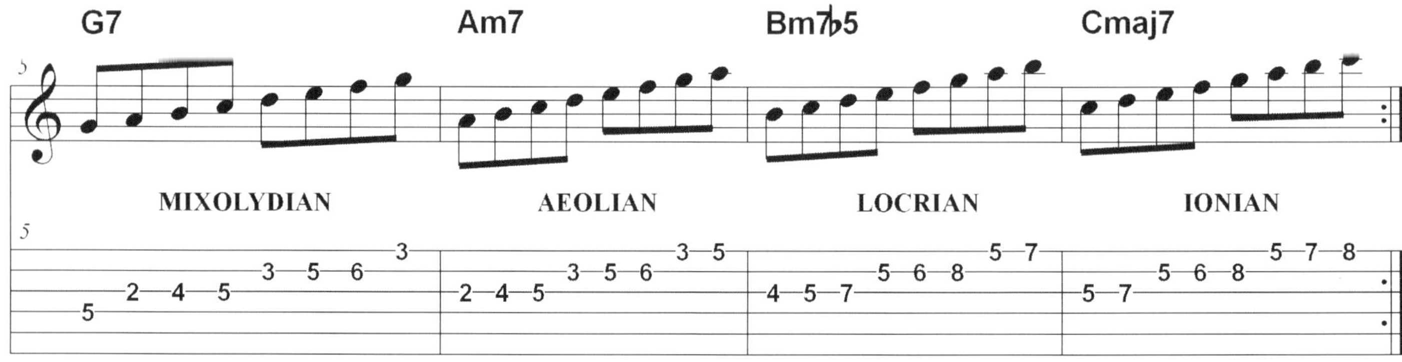

Example 8

Track 6

In this example we play the Dorian mode **(D-E-F-G-A-B-C-D)** on Dm7 and the Mixolydian mode **(G-A-B-C-D-E-F-G)** on G7 within a ii-V-I progression, the most common chord progression in jazz.

Example 9

Track 7

As in the previous example, we again use the Dorian and Mixolydian modes on the same progression.
Try composing similar examples of your own.

PENTATONIC SCALES

As the name indicates, pentatonic scales are made up of 5 tones. Any scale reduced to 5 tones could be called a pentatonic scale. These scales are very effective when improvising melodically. They are divided into natural and artificial pentatonic scales. The most common in our musical system are the so-called **major and minor pentatonic scales** belonging to the group of **natural pentatonics**, since they are derived from the Ionian and Aeolian modes. These scales are characterized by the absence of the semitones that define the major and natural minor scales, so they are good against either the Ionian (major) or Aeolian (pure minor) modes.

THE C MAJOR PENTATONIC SCALE

This scale is obtained by omitting degrees 4 and 7 of the major (Ionian) scale, and has the following interval structure: major second, major second, minor third, major second, minor third.

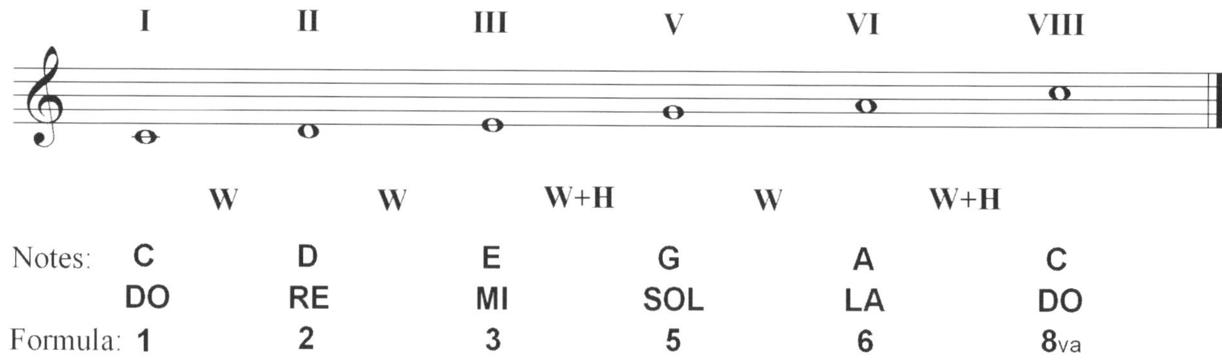

THE A MINOR PENTATONIC SCALE

This scale is obtained by omitting degrees 2 and 6 of the natural minor scale (Aeolian). Like the natural minor scale that is derived from the major scale, the minor pentatonic is a mode derived from the major pentatonic, but in this case, building it from the fifth note of the major pentatonic. This scale is composed of intervals of major seconds and minor thirds. Note that the member notes of the two scales are identical; only the tonic notes and interval placements are different.

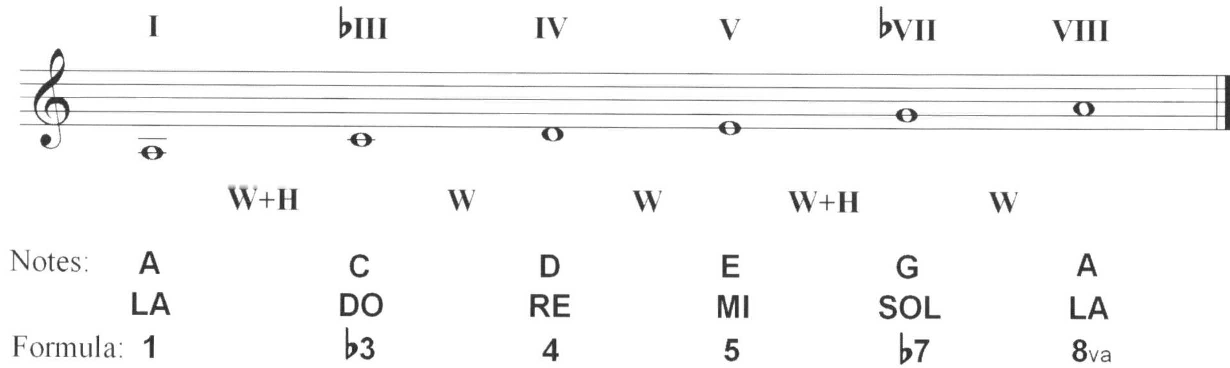

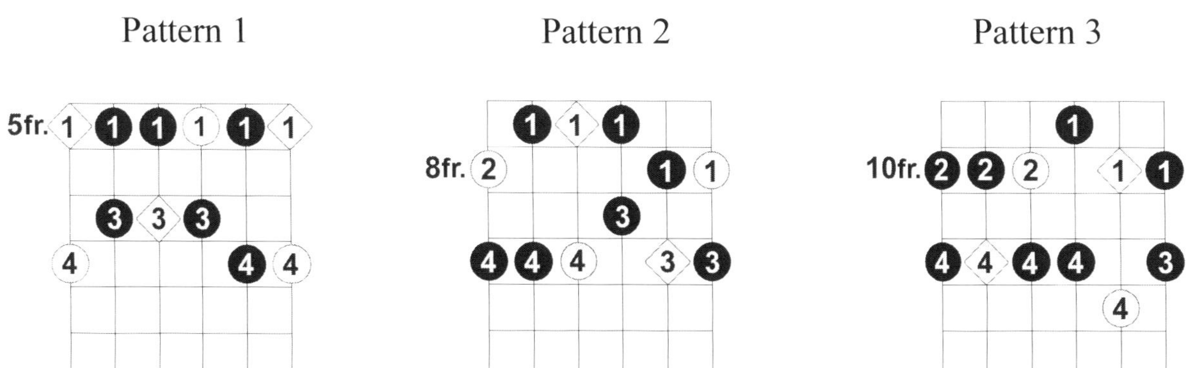

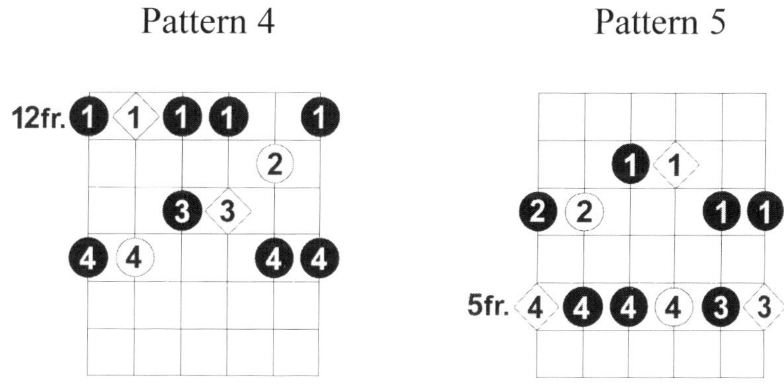

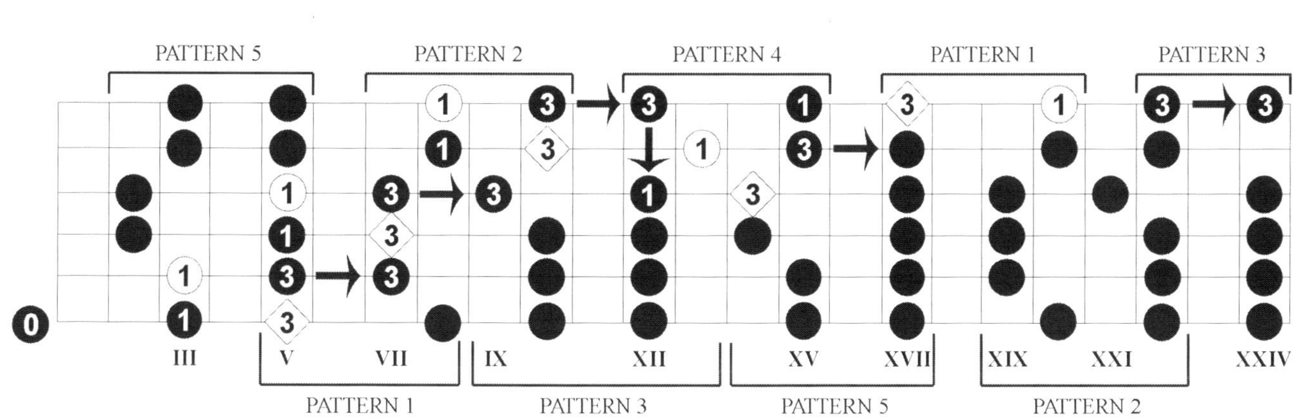

◇ The diamonds indicate the A minor tonics.

○ The white circles indicate the C major tonics.

Notice that in pattern 1, your index finger is on the minor tonic (A), and your pinky is on the relative major tonic (C) on strings 1 and 6.
Use this handy guide to play pentatonic scales in any minor or major key.
The hexatonic (6-tone) blues scale is made up of the minor pentatonic plus the ♭5 (or ♯4) of the original heptatonic (7-tone) minor scale: A – C – D – D♯ – E – G – A.

(See the application of pentatonic scales in the Modern Blues chapter.)

HARMONIZING THE MAJOR SCALE WITH TRIADS

We can form a 3-note chord on each note of the major scale by superimposing or **stacking** two consecutive diatonic thirds; for example, if we use the note C as the first degree of the scale, the first third to be superimposed will be E and the second will be G—forming the major chord or triad (C-E-G). If we perform the same procedure starting from the second degree of the scale, that is, D—the first third to be superimposed will be F while the second will be A—thus forming the minor chord or triad (D-F-A), and so on with the other degrees of the scale.
The lowest note in the chord (based on the scale degree) is called the **tonic, root** or **fundamental** (1) and is the tone that gives us the name of the chord. The next note, an interval of a third away from the tonic (3) is called the **third** of the chord. The third of the chord can be either major or minor. It is **major** when it is two whole steps away from the tonic and **minor** when it is 1 and 1/2 steps away from the tonic. The **fifth** of the chord (5) can be **perfect, diminished** or **augmented**. The fifth is **perfect** when it is 3 and 1/2 steps away from the tonic, **diminished** when it is 3 whole-steps away from the tonic, and **augmented** when it is 4 whole-steps away from the tonic.

By means of the previously explained procedure of stacking thirds, here are the chords generated by scale tones in the key of C major. Chord locations within the scale are traditionally indicated with Roman numerals.

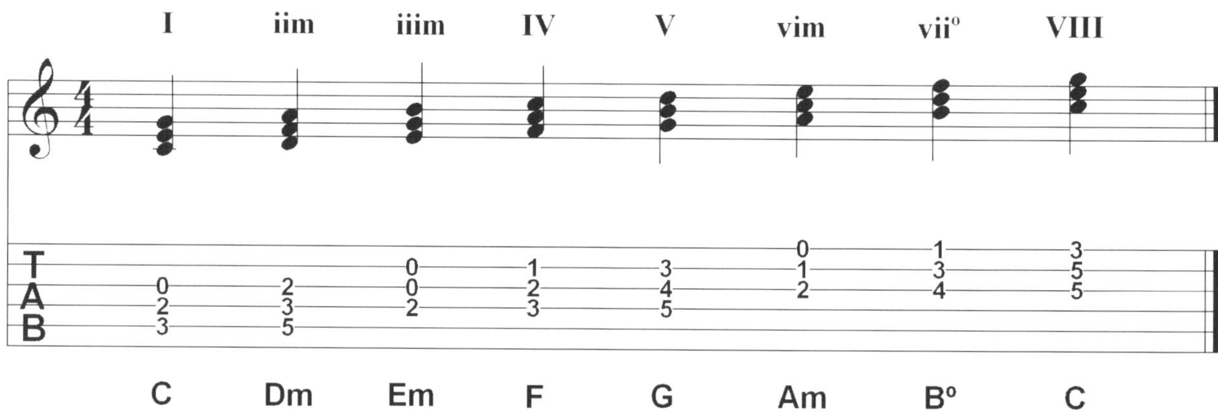

The triads generated by the major scale are grouped in three categories:

1. MAJOR CHORDS **(I-IV-V)**

Formed by the tonic, the major third and the perfect fifth, major triads can also be built by combining the tonic with a major third and a minor third.

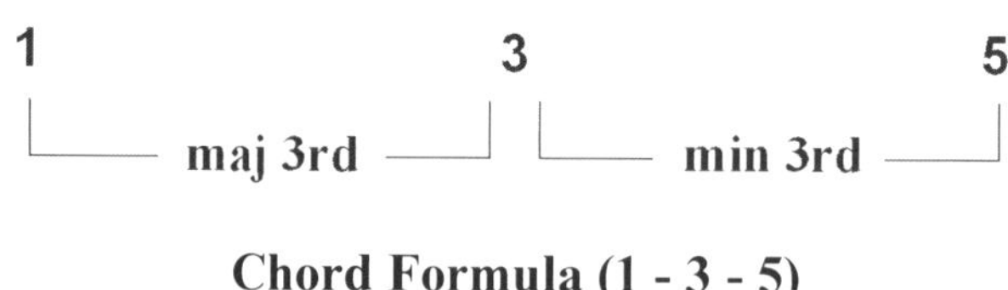

Chord Formula (1 - 3 - 5)

2. MINOR CHORDS **(ii-iii-vi)**

Minor triads are formed by the tonic, the minor third and the perfect fifth. They can also be built by combining a minor third and a major third.

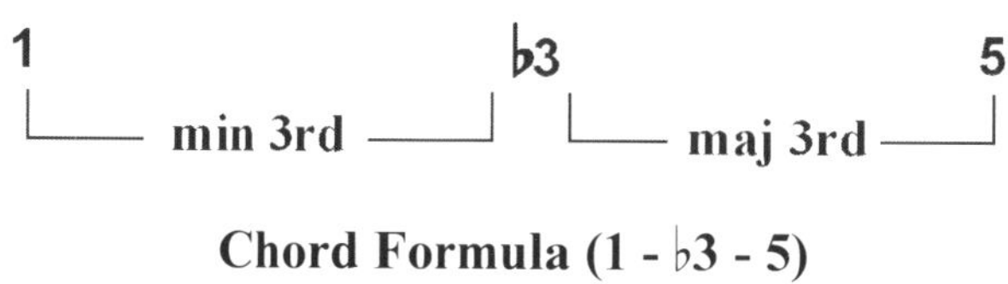

Chord Formula (1 - ♭3 - 5)

3. DIMINISHED CHORD (vii°)

Formed by the tonic, the minor third and the diminished or flat-fifth; They can also be built by combining 2 minor thirds.

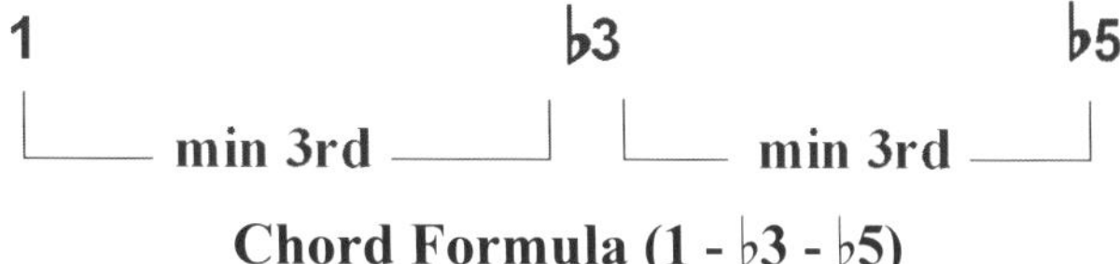

Chord Formula (1 - ♭3 - ♭5)

In all major keys, the major, minor and diminished triads occur in the following order:

I	ii	iii	IV	V	vi	vii°	VIII
Major	Minor	Minor	Major	Major	Minor	Diminished	Major

HARMONIZING THE MAJOR SCALE WITH 7th CHORDS

Seventh chords are the result of superimposing or stacking one more interval of a third on top of a triad, forming a 4-note chord; seventh (7th) chords are also known as **quad chords**. This new sound is named for the interval formed between the fundamental or root of the chord and the added note seven notes up from the tonic, counting the tonic as I.

If we consider C as the fundamental note of the chord, its seventh degree will be B. If we think of D as the fundamental note of the chord, its seventh degree will be C, and so on with the other degrees of the key. Remember that the seventh is **major** when it is a half-step away from the tonic, **minor** when it is a whole step away from the tonic and **diminished** when it is 1 and 1/2 steps away from the tonic.

Here are the 4-note chords generated by the key of C major:

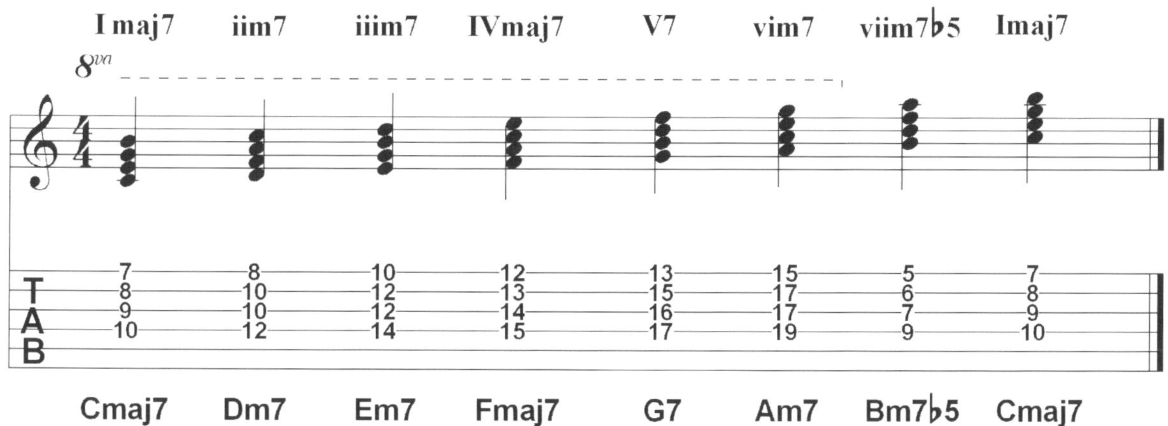

We can group these chords into four categories:

1) MAJOR SEVENTH CHORDS

These chords are made up of the tonic, the major third, the perfect fifth, and the major seventh.

Position within the scale	Symbol	Formula
I and IV	maj7, △	1, 3, 5, 7

2) MINOR SEVENTH CHORDS

These chords are made up of the tonic, the minor third, the perfect fifth, and the minor seventh.

Position within the scale	Symbol	Formula
ii, iii and vi	m7, -7	1, ♭3, 5, ♭7

3) MAJOR CHORD WITH MINOR SEVENTH (Dominant 7th)

This chord is formed by the tonic, the major third, the perfect fifth and the minor seventh and is known as the **dominant seventh** chord, because it is based on the fifth or dominant degree of the scale.

Position within the scale	Symbol	Formula
V	7	1, 3, 5, ♭7

4) MINOR CHORD WITH MINOR SEVENTH AND DIMINISHED FIFTH:

This chord is formed by the tonic, the minor third, the diminished fifth and the minor seventh and is known as a **minor 7th flat-5** or **half-diminished seventh** chord.

Position within the scale	Symbol	Formula
vii	m7♭5, ø	1, ♭3, ♭5, ♭7

Note that the **fully diminished seventh** chord would lower the 7th by another half tone: 1, ♭3, ♭5, ♭♭7.
As the intervals between member notes of this chord are all minor thirds, this chord can be named from any of its member notes. As the double flat does not naturally occur in the diatonic major scale, we will not give fully diminished seventh chords more attention here. Just know that they exit and have their own unique sound and purpose.

In all major keys, the 7th chords occur in the following order:

I	ii	iii	IV	V	vi	vii°	VIII
maj7	m7	m7	maj7	7	m7	m7♭5	maj7

The following table shows the 4-note chords on the scale degrees of all major scales.

KEY	I	ii	iii	IV	V7	vi	vii	VIII
C	Cmaj7	Dm7	Em7	Fmaj7	G7	Am7	Bm7♭5	Cmaj7
F	Fmaj7	Gm7	Am7	B♭maj7	C7	Dm7	Em7♭5	Fmaj7
B♭	B♭maj7	Cm7	Dm7	E♭maj7	F7	Gm7	Am7♭5	B♭maj7
E♭	E♭maj7	Fm7	Gm7	A♭maj7	B♭7	Cm7	Dm7♭5	E♭maj7
A♭	A♭maj7	B♭m7	Cm7	D♭maj7	E♭7	Fm7	Gm7♭5	A♭maj7
D♭	D♭maj7	E♭m7	Fm7	G♭maj7	A♭7	B♭m7	Cm7♭5	D♭maj7
G♭	G♭maj7	A♭m7	B♭m7	C♭maj7	D♭7	E♭m7	Fm7♭5	G♭maj7
B	Bmaj7	C♯m7	D♯m7	Emaj7	F♯7	G♯m7	A♯m7♭5	Bmaj7
E	Emaj7	F♯m7	G♯m7	Amaj7	B7	C♯m7	D♯m7♭5	Emaj7
A	Amaj7	Bm7	C♯m7	Dmaj7	E7	F♯m7	G♯m7♭5	Amaj7
D	Amaj7	Em7	F♯m7	Gmaj7	A7	Bm7	C♯m7♭5	Dmaj7
G	Gmaj7	Am7	Bm7	Cmaj7	D7	Em7	F♯m7♭5	Gmaj7

ADDING NOTES TO 7th CHORDS

Until now, we have seen that chords can be made up of 3 or 4 tones; 3-note chords have been formed with degrees 1, 3 and 5 of the scale, while 4-note chords have been formed with degrees 1, 3, 5 and 7. Now, in addition to these tones, we can add other notes of the scale, usually by stacking intervals of a third. These notes generally exceed one octave; for example, 9 (ninth), 11 (eleventh), and 13 (thirteenth) chords are equivalent to intervals of a second (2), fourth (4) and sixth (6) respectively—but one octave higher. Note that if we tried to add an interval of a fifteenth (15), we would simply reach the tonic again, so 13 (thirteenth) is as far as a 7th chord can be extended.

It is important to keep in mind that by adding these notes we would not modify the specific function of the chords, but rather the added tones would provide a different **color** and enrich the harmony of the moment.

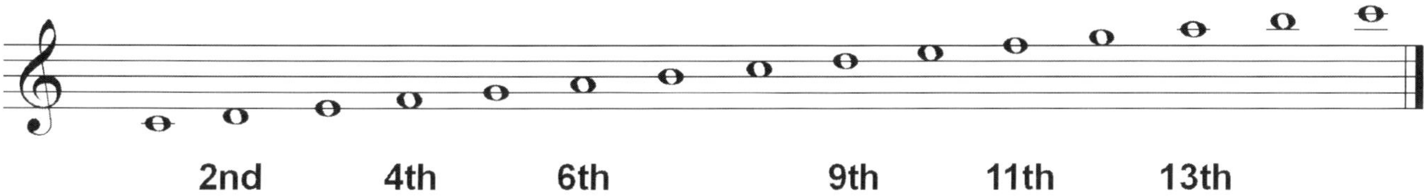

EXTENSIONS OF THE DOMINANT SEVENTH CHORD

The tones that can be added to the dominant seventh chord can be divided into two groups:

a) Addition of the ninth (9), the eleventh (11) and the thirteenth (13); these notes provide a calm and serene Mixolydian sound.

b) Addition of the flat-9 (♭9), the augmented ninth (♯9) and the augmented 5th (♯5); these tones create dissonance that requires a **resolution**. They are generally called **tension notes** or simply **tensions**. Keep in mind that tensions lie outside the diatonic mixolydian scale. In certain cases, tensions create a jazzier sonority.

CHORD GRIDS FOR EXTENSIONS OF DOMINANT 7ths

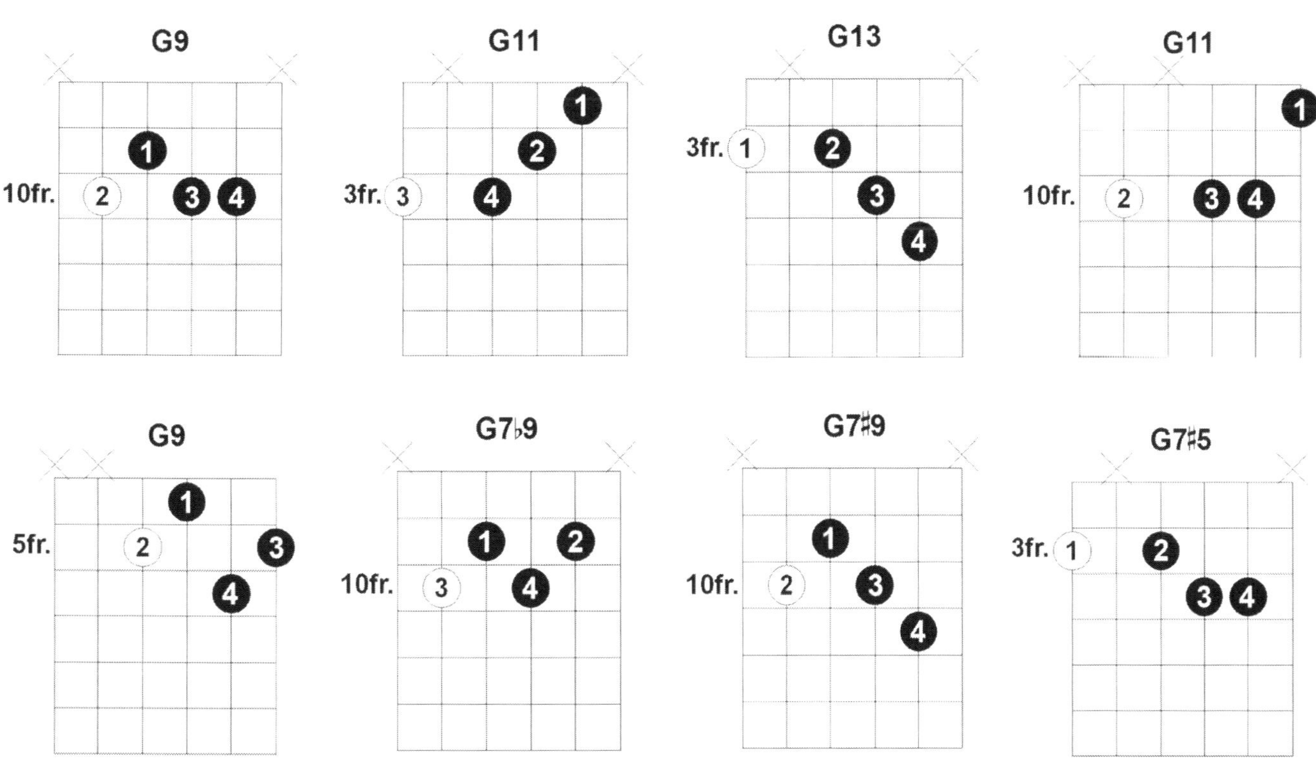

CHAPTER 2
Rhythmic Aspects of Soloing

Rhythm was the first musically artistic manifestation of primitive man, using different sounds at different pitches and durations. We can define rhythm as the relationship between the inception and duration of sounds. The correct duration of the sound is determined by the figure that represents it. In modern standard notation, there are seven symbols or figures whose shape and denomination represent the duration of a sound.

The following table shows the relative value of rhythm symbols in the form of a pyramid. You can see that each figure is worth twice the time value of the following one but just half of the previous one; for example, a half note is worth half of a whole note but equivalent to the value of 2 quarter notes, and a quarter note is worth half of a half note but equal to 2 tied eighth notes.

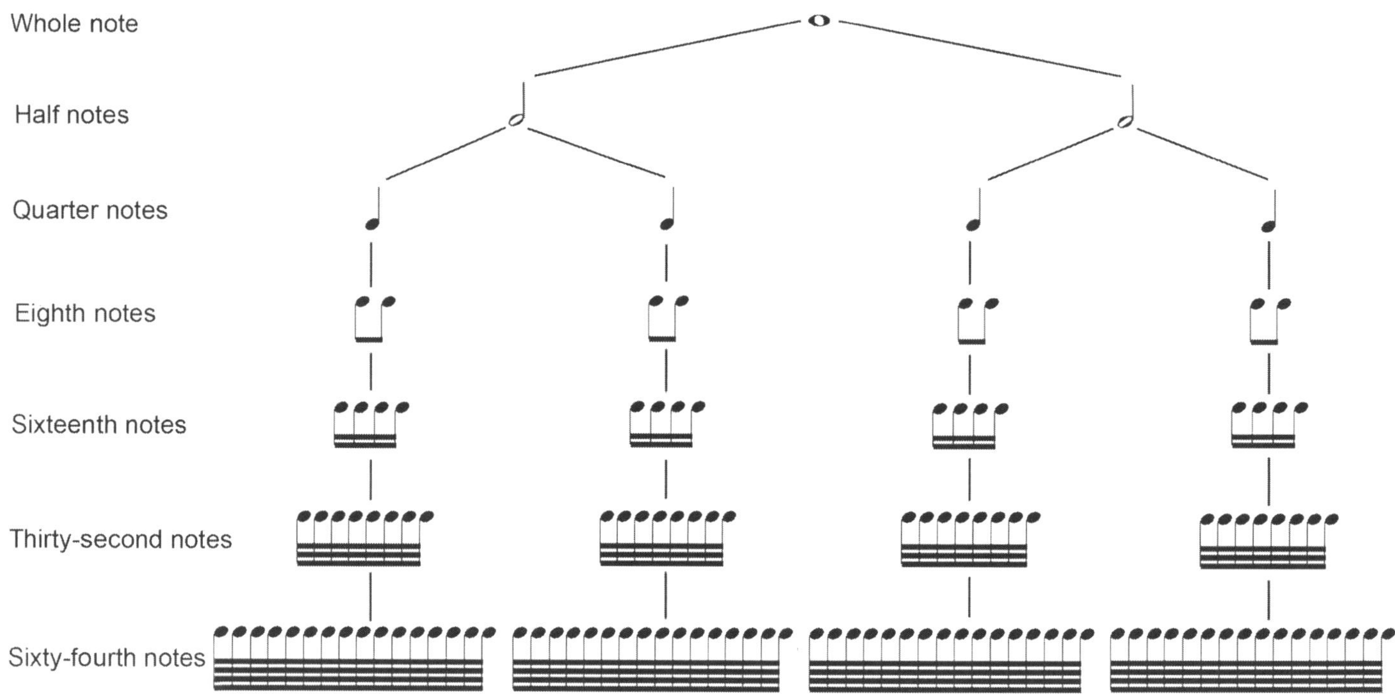

Next, we will practice playing the main rhythmic figures.

For a better understanding of rhythm, it is advisable to first sing each figure in solfege syllables while conducting yourself with basic patterns; alternatively, you could count time aloud (1-and-2-and etc.) marking time with your foot and clapping the rhythms. Ultimately, you could play along with the recordings.
It is important to comprehend each rhythm figure before moving on to the next one.

Track 8

a. Whole Note

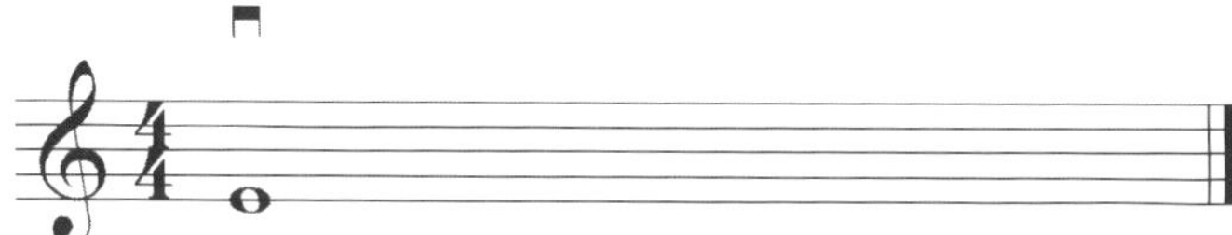

b. Half Notes

c. Quarter Notes

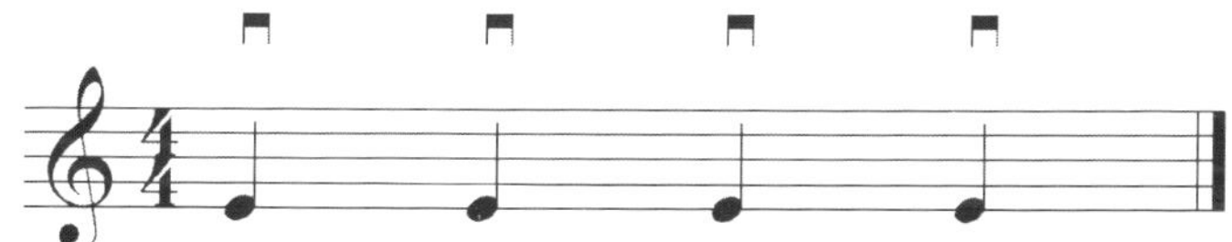

d. Eighth Notes

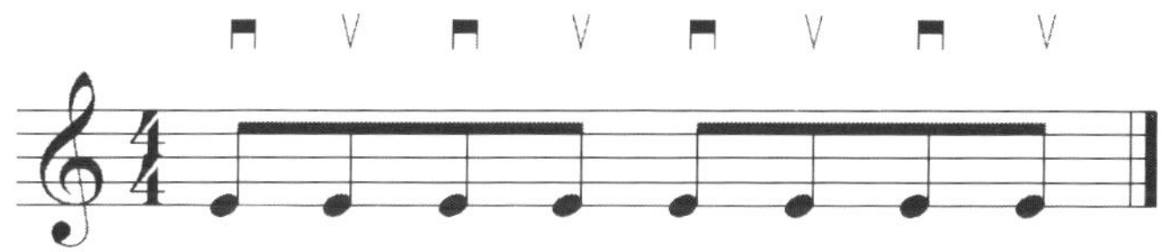

e. Sixteenth Notes

f. Triplet Eighth Notes

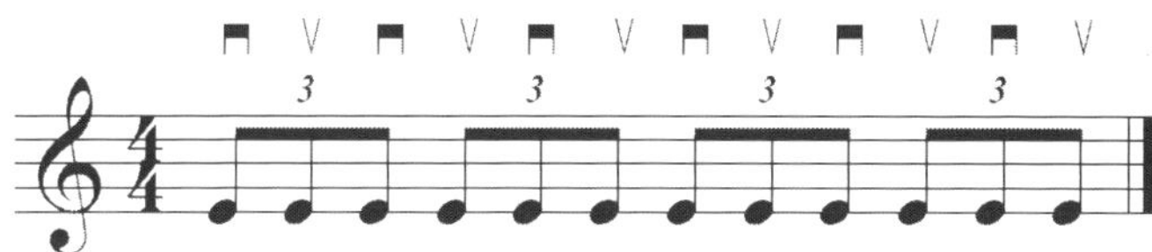

g. Quintuplet Sixteenth Notes

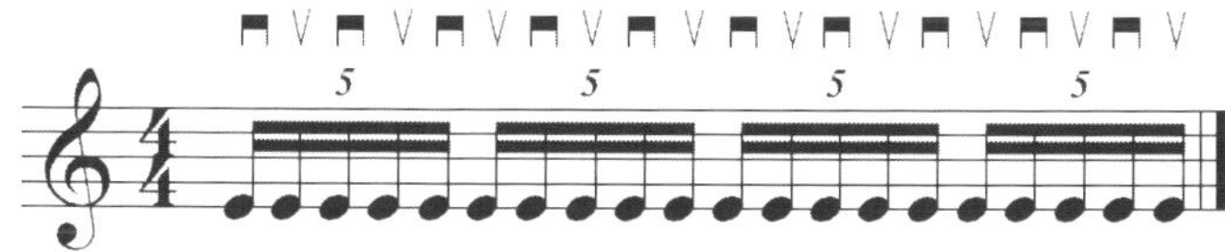

h. Sextuplet Sixteenth Notes

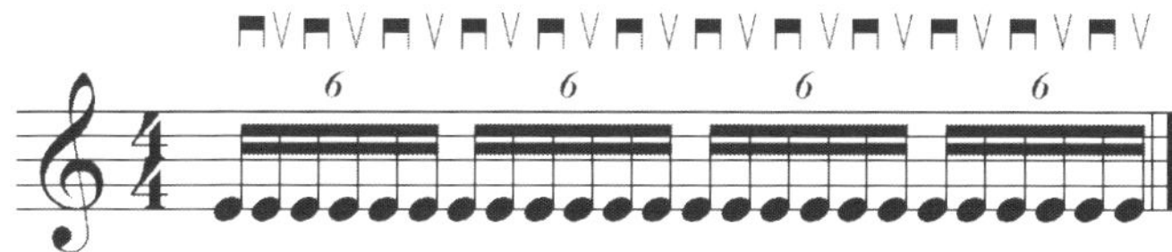

i. Septuplet Sixteenth Notes

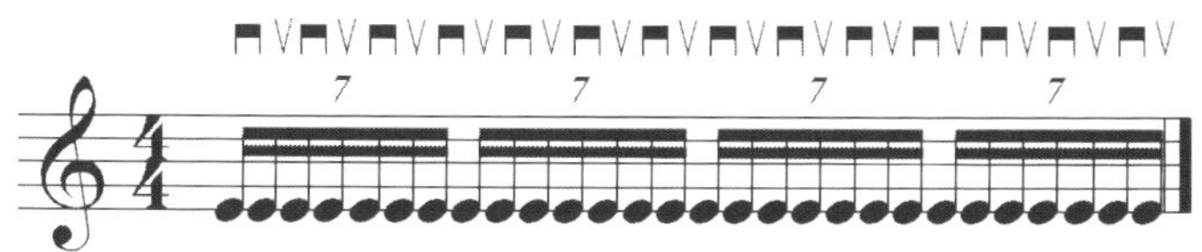

j. Thirty-Second Notes

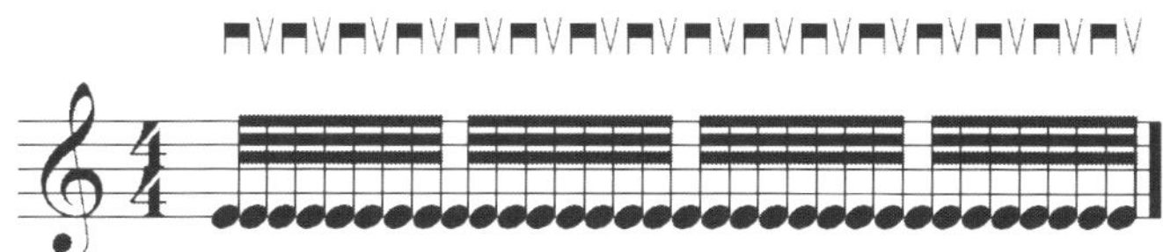

ACCENTS

Accents or the attack of certain notes with more intensity than others—are a very important part of musical performance. An accent is represented by the following symbol: >

Here are some exercises that incorporate this concept. You can invent similar examples and, of course—incorporate them in your solos.

Practice accentuation in various rhythmic figures.

Track 9

Example 10

Quarter Notes

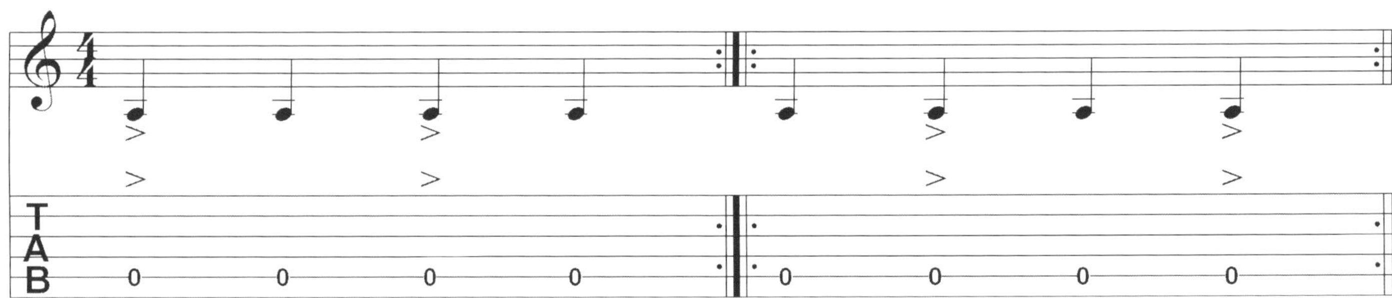

Example 11

Eighth Notes

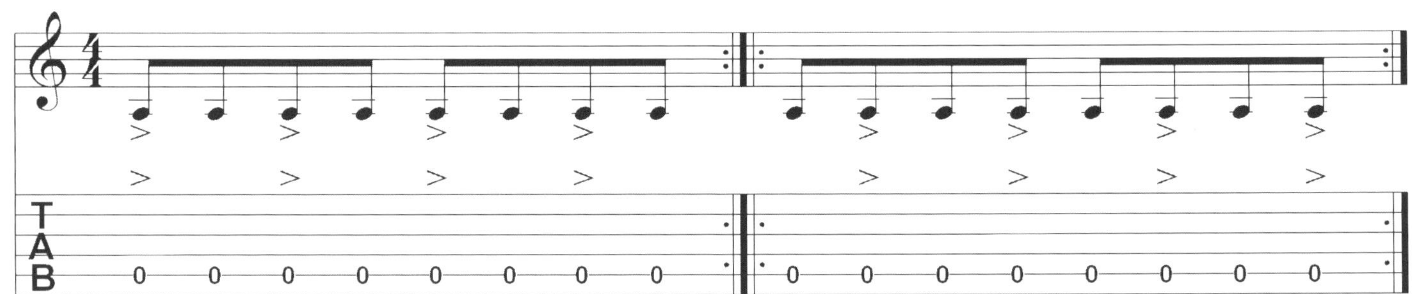

Example 12

Triplet Eighth Notes

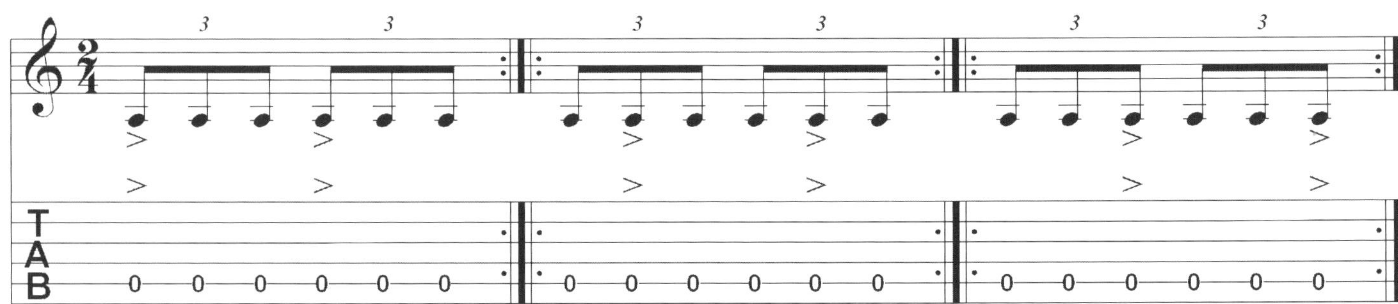

Example 13

Sixteenth Notes

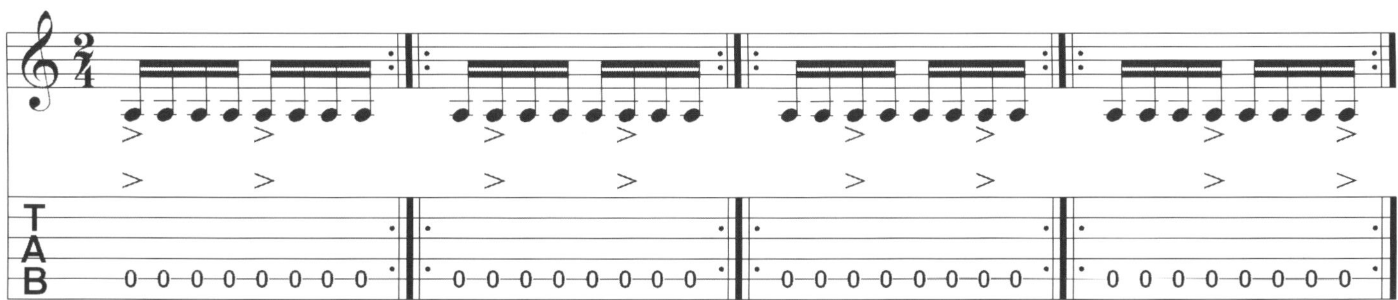

The following examples illustrate different combinations of eighth notes, dotted eighth notes and sixteenth notes.

Listen carefully to each example.

DOTTED EIGHTH AND SIXTEENTH NOTES

Track 10

It is important that you play and experiment with all possible rhythm combinations. Write them down, sing them and then apply them to your instrument.

Example 14

DYNAMICS

In music, when we talk about dynamics, we are referring to the graduation of the intensity or volume of the sound, the quality that allows us to differentiate a soft sound from a loud one. These changes in volume give expression and movement to the music. Playing everything at the same level of intensity produces only a boring and monotonous interpretation.
Traditionally, dynamics are indicated with abbreviations of Italian terms like ***p*** for ***piano*** (soft) and ***f*** for ***forte*** (loud). From these two dynamics, other variations are used to indicate the desired volume level more precisely.

pp	pianissimo	very soft
p	piano	soft
mp	mezzo piano	moderately soft
mf	mezzo forte	moderately loud
f	forte	loud
ff	fortissimo	very loud
sfp	sforzando piano	very loud, followed by soft

Track 11

Example 15

In the first example we start by playing ***pianissimo*** in the first measure and then come down with a ***forte*** on the second measure.

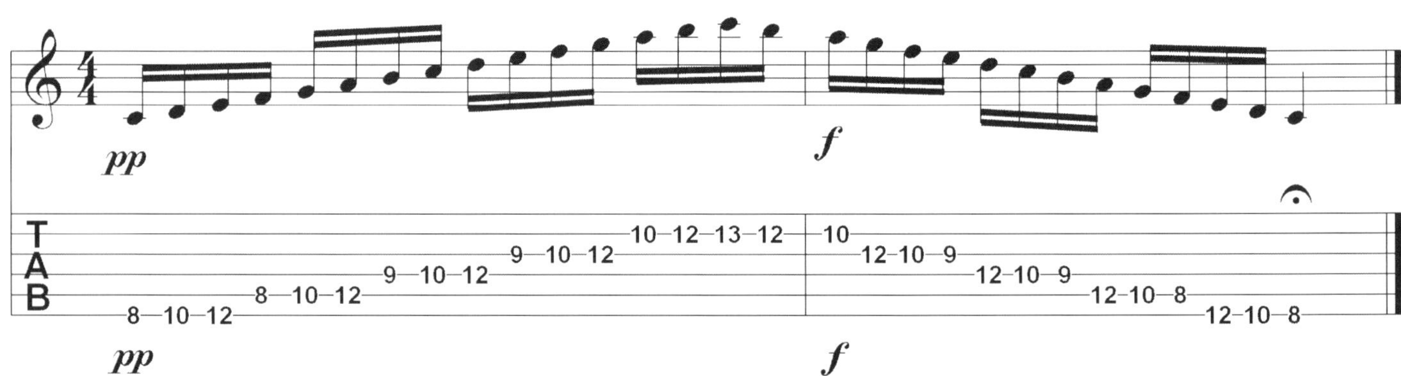

Example 16

Now we go the other way, ascending with a ***forte*** and descending with a ***pianissimo***.

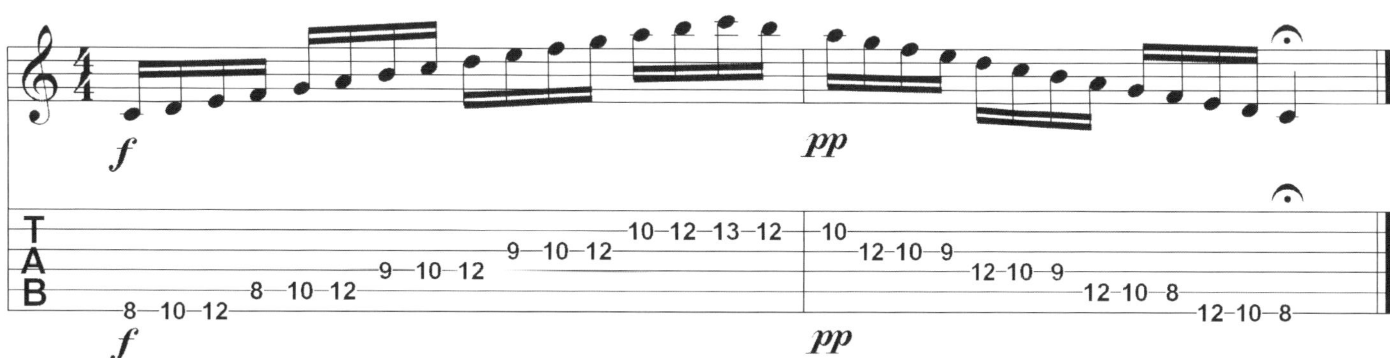

There are also symbols that tell us to move gradually from one dynamic level to another. These markings are formally called **regulators** but also known as "hairpins" for obvious reasons:

Crescendo - gradually getting louder

Decrescendo - gradually getting softer

Example 17

In the following example we start from a ***pianissimo*** and perform a **crescendo** until we reach a ***fortissimo***; then we perform a **diminuendo**, gradually returning to playing ***pianissimo***.

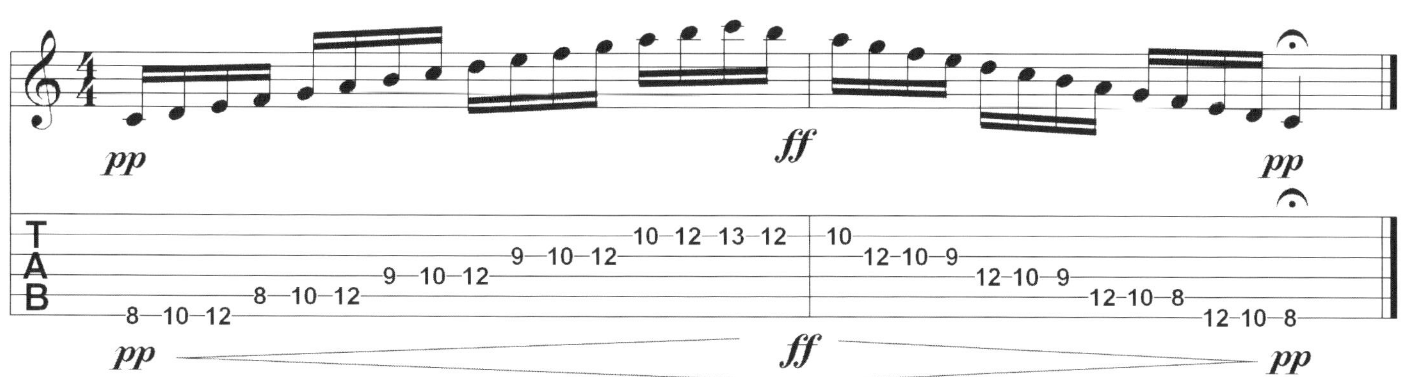

Example 18

Now we start from a ***fortissimo*** and perform a **diminuendo** until we reach a ***pianissimo***; then we perform a **crescendo** until we return to playing ***fortissimo***.

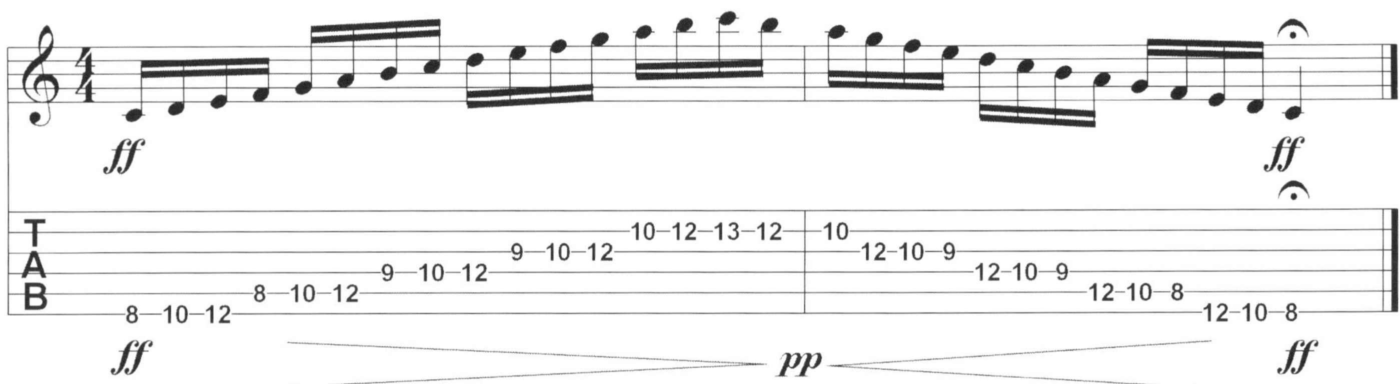

In the following examples we will see how dynamics work within a musical phrase.

Example 19

Track 12

In the next phrase, we start by playing soft and perform a **crescendo** until we reach a ***forte***. Then in the third measure we play a **diminuendo** until we reach a ***piano***.

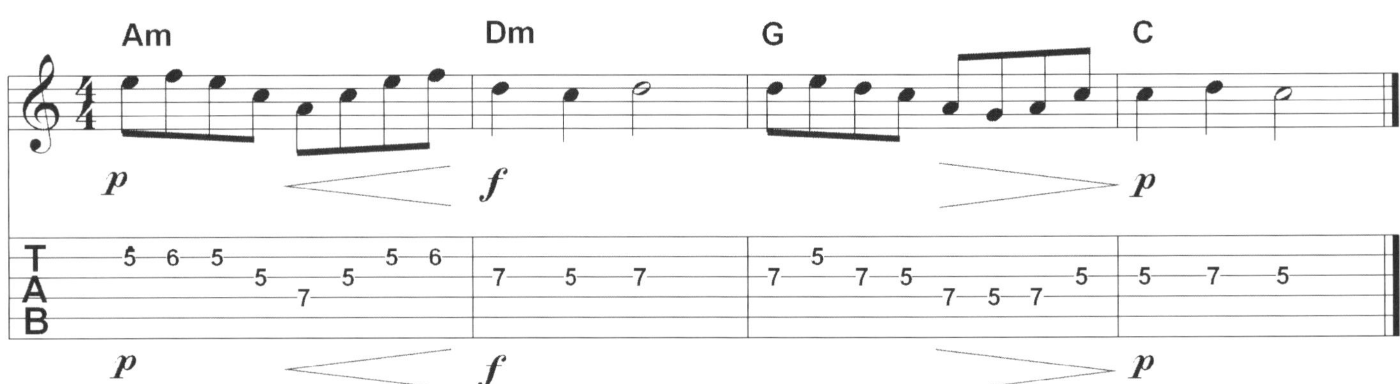

Example 20

Track 13

Here, we start from a ***pianissimo*** and perform a **crescendo** until we reach a ***fortissimo***. In the third measure we begin a **diminuendo,** ultimately returning to ***pianissimo***.

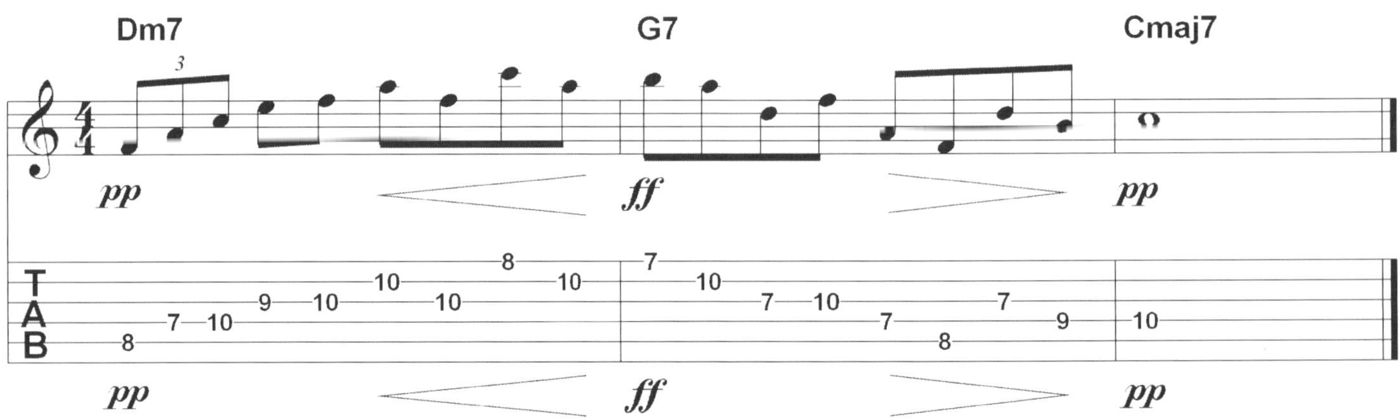

It is **very** important that you integrate the concept of changing dynamics into your own music. One approach is to listen to classical music and appreciate the changes in the intensity of sound.

6/8 TIME

A measure of 6/8 time is said to be a **compound measure**. Compound measures have the numerators 6, 9 or 12 which are **ternary**, that is, divisible by three and represented by dotted figures. In a measure of 6/8 time, the dotted quarter note and dotted quarter rest are used only on beats 1 and 4; repeated eighth notes and rests are used wherever quarter notes and rests would create hard to read syncopations. In modern practice, the symbol for a tone lasting a full measure of 6/8 is the dotted half note, whereas **the symbol for a full measure of silence is a whole rest, whatever the time signature.**

A measure of 6/8 is counted and conducted as a binary measure with 2 beats, each with a ternary subdivision of 3 eighth notes per beat—a truly compound measure. The first beat of the measure is considered strong with a lesser emphasis on beat 4; the other beats are weak.
The 6/8 time signature is often used in progressive rock, heavy metal, blues and other styles.

Here are some common rhythms in 6/8 meter:

Listen carefully to each example and when you are ready, create your own rhythm combinations. Be sure to write them down!

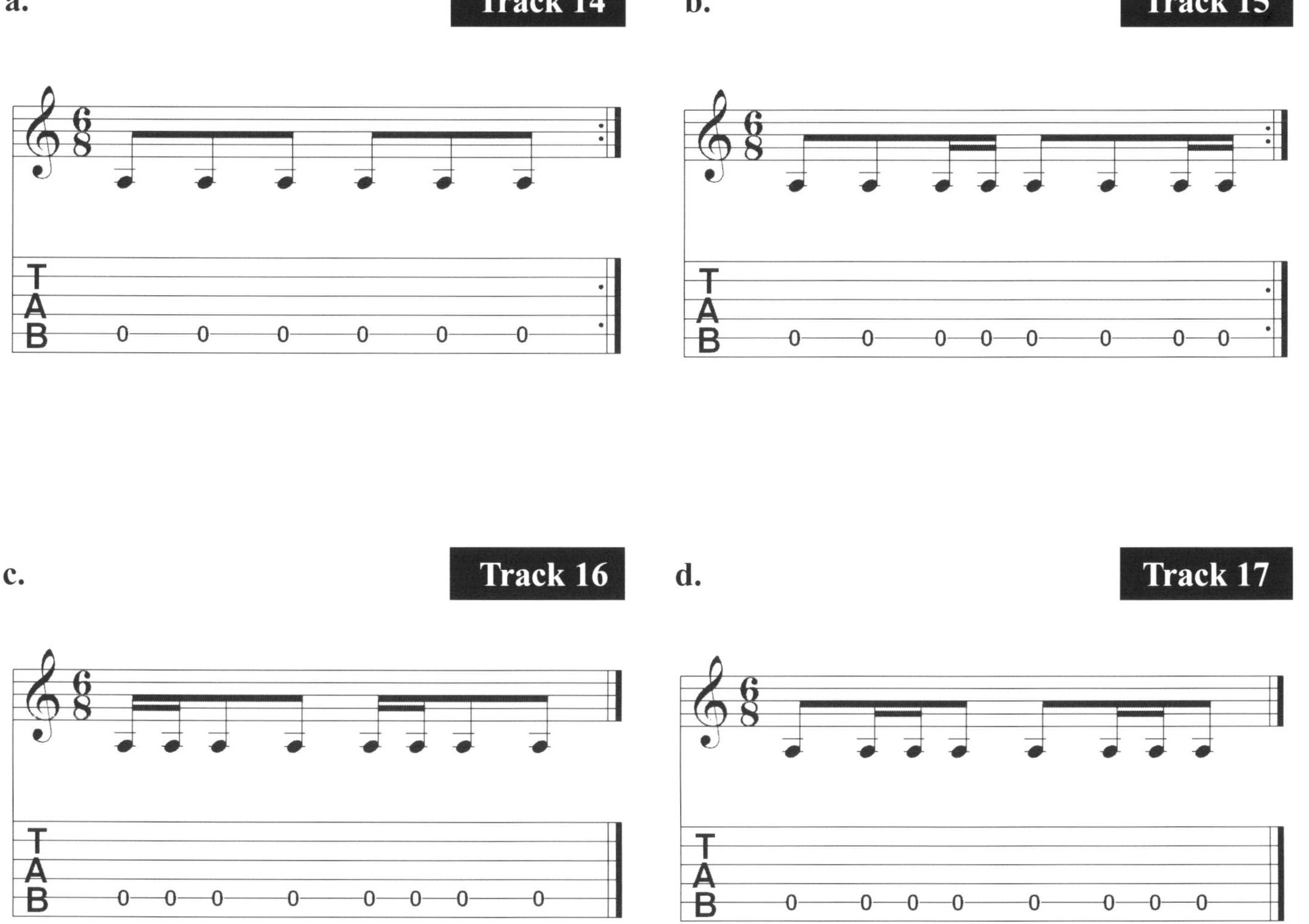

e. **Track 18**

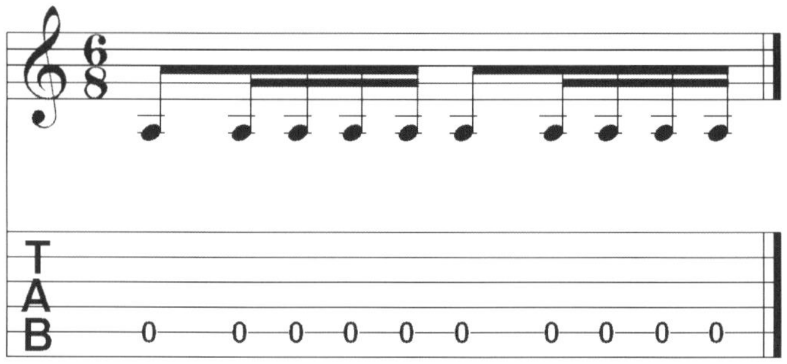

f. **Track 19**

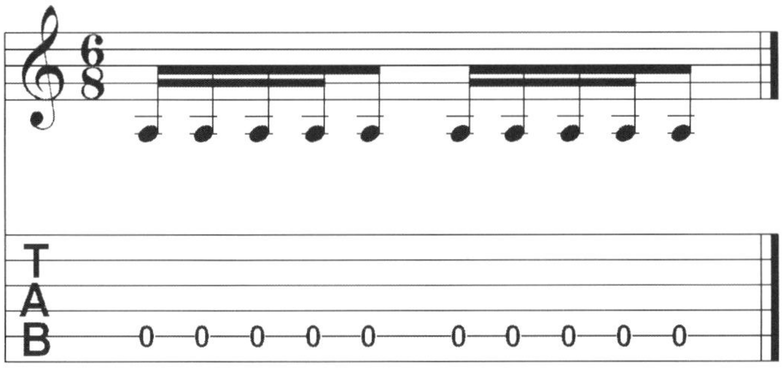

g. **Track 20**

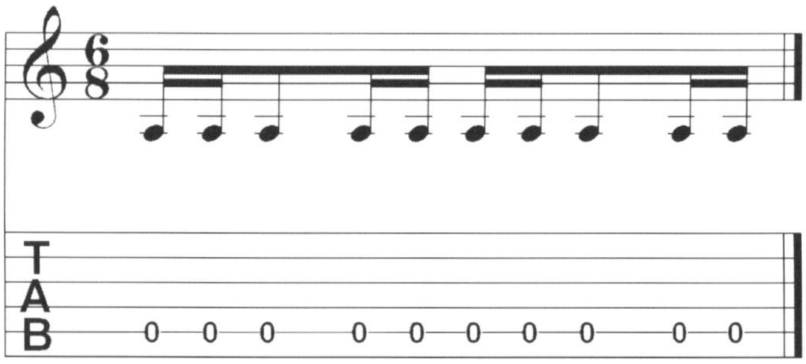

h. **Track 21**

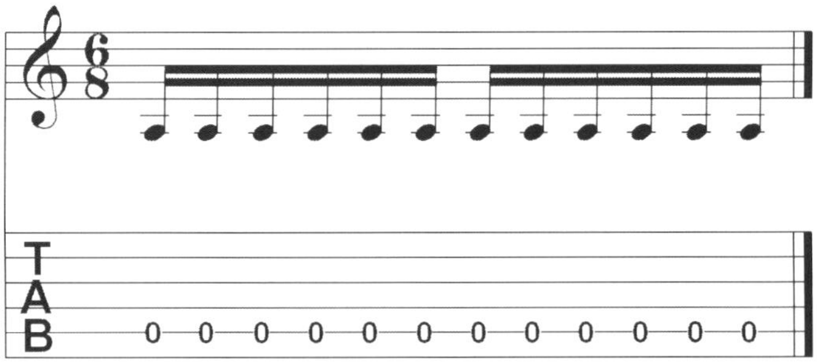

i. **Track 22**

j. **Track 23**

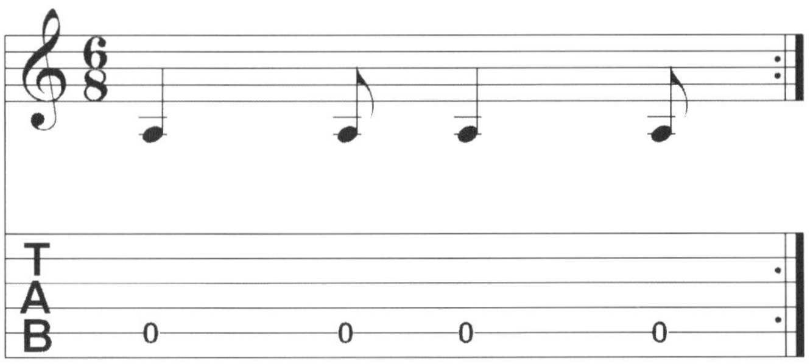

Here are examples of 6/8 rhythms in a more musical context:

Example 21

Track 24

The following sample is built on the E minor pentatonic scale: **E-G-A-B-D**. Here, we play rhythm Examples **d.** and **a.**

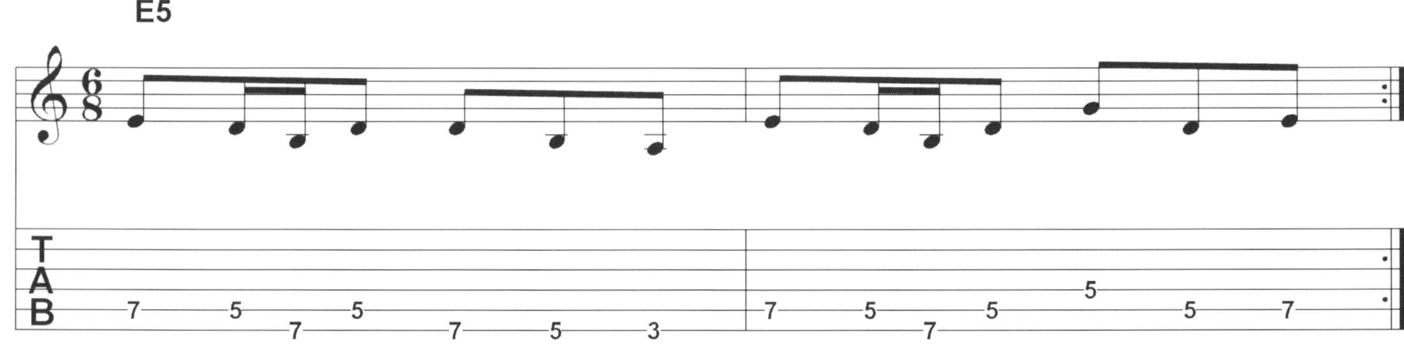

Example 22

Track 25

The next progression uses rhythms **d.** and **e.** with the A pure minor scale: **A-B-C-D-E-F-G-A**.

Example 23

Track 26

Now we will work with rhythms **e.** and **a.** using the natural Am scale.

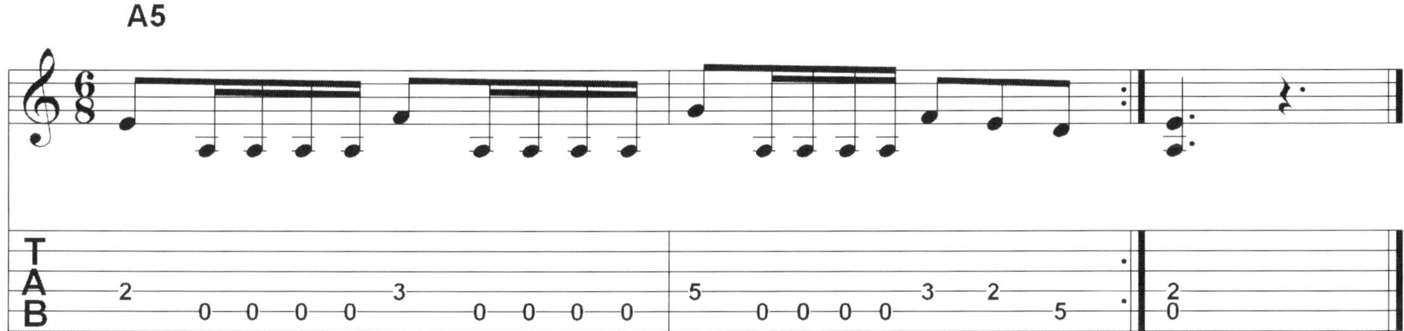

Example 24

Track 27

In the following example we combine Examples **b.** and **h.** using the Am pentatonic scale **A-C-D-E-G**.

Example 25

Track 28

In this last 6/8 example we apply various rhythm figures over an Am progression.
Pay attention to the rests in the last measure.

7/8 TIME

Seven-eight time is one of the so-called **odd** or **asymmetrical meters**, which means the main beats of the measure have different durations. This measure has no even divisions but contains three principal beats, two beats being of a quarter note and one of a dotted quarter note value. Given this characteristic, we can distribute the beats in 3 different ways:

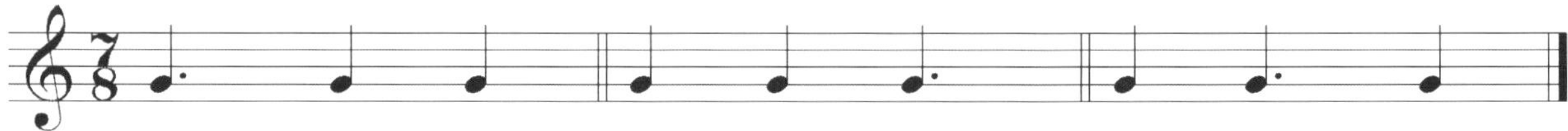

In the following example we subdivide each main beat of the measure into 7 equal eighth notes.

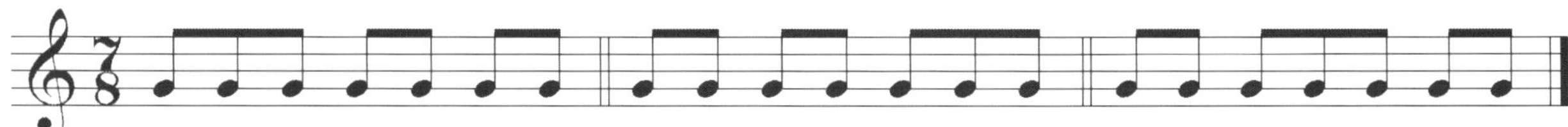

As you can see, these measures have two different types of beats, one with three eighth notes and the others with two eighth notes. In each case, the three-eighth-note beat has a duration of a dotted quarter note, while the two eighth-note beats have a duration of one quarter note. It is also possible to subdivide the eighth notes into sixteenth notes, giving rise to several possible combinations. **This type of measure is very common in progressive rock, fusion and metal styles.**

Below are some common eighth/quarter/dotted-quarter combinations in 7/8 meter. Listen carefully to each example and when you are ready, create your own combinations, write them down and then play them!

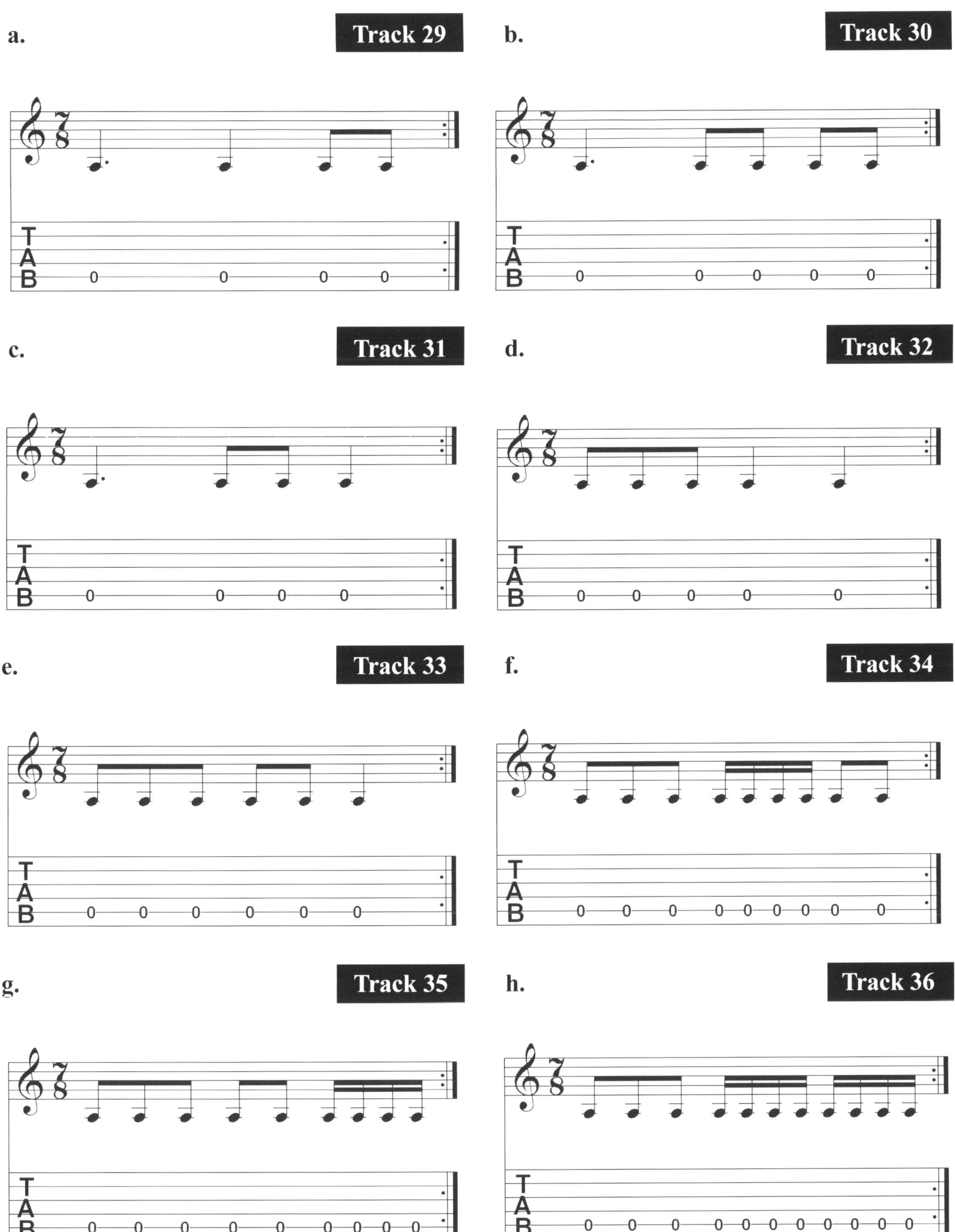

Now let's look at some examples of 7/8 meter in a musical context.

Example 26

Track 37

This first example combines examples **g.** and **h.** using the A pure minor scale: **A-B-C-D-E-F-G-A**.

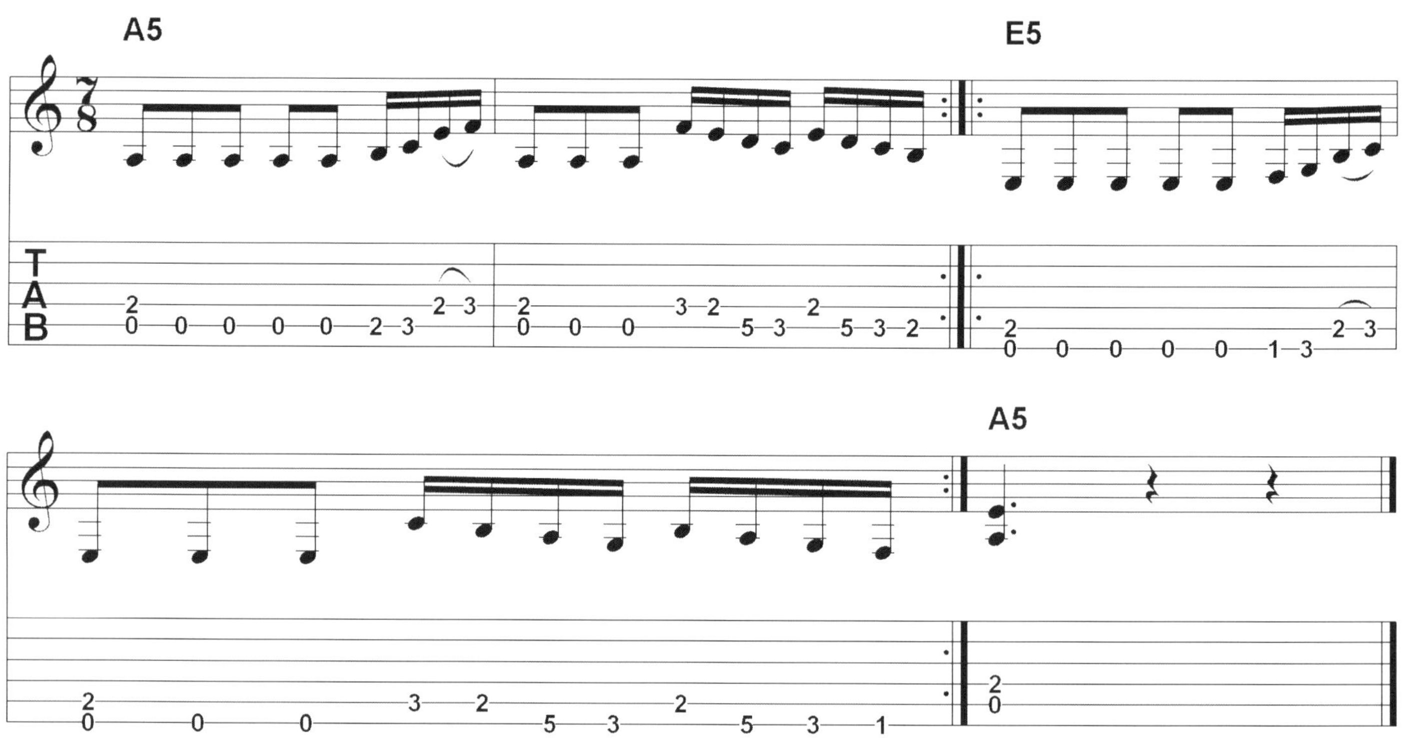

Example 27

Track 38

In the following *riff* we combine examples **a.** and **d.** in the key of Am.

Example 28

Track 39

Finally, here is example **f.** combined with a riff built on the Phrygian mode: **E-F-G-A-B-C-D-E**.

AMALGAM MEASURES

Amalgam measures are created by combining two or more simple or compound measures. **Simple amalgam measures** are those with numerators of **5, 7 and 9.**

A measure of 5/4 time is formed by alternating a measure of 3/4 with a measure of 2/4 time.

A measure of 7/4 time is formed by alternating a measure of 4/4 time with one of 3/4 time.

A measure of 9/4 time is formed by a measure of 4 beats, plus one of 3 beats and another of 2 beats.

These types of meters are often found in progressive rock and metal.

Example 29 **Track 40**

In this example of **5/4** time, we use the E minor pentatonic scale: **E-G-A-B-D**.

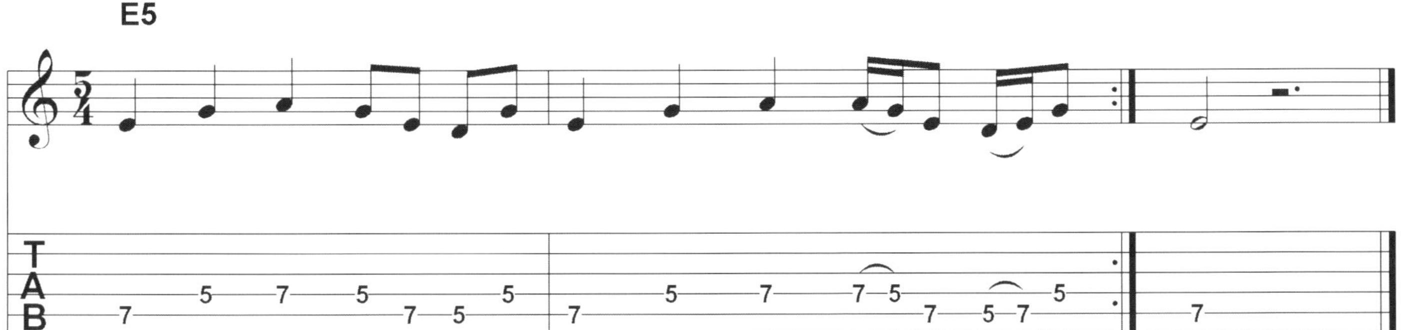

Example 30 **Track 41**

Here, in a new phrase in **5/4** time we again work with the E minor pentatonic scale, this time in first position. It's interesting to use open strings to create rock and blues phrases.

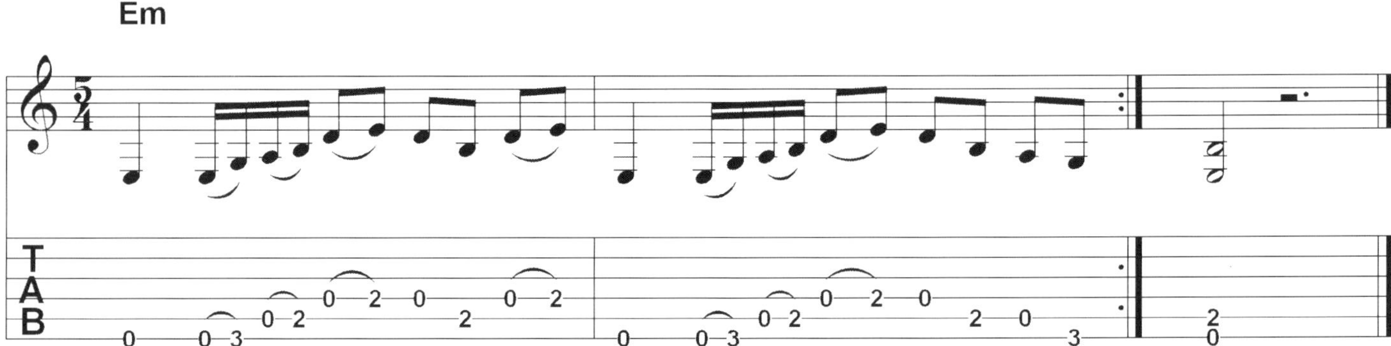

Example 31 **Track 42**

Now we'll work on **7/4** time. In this meter we alternate a 4/4 measure with a 3/4 measure. The following riff is built on the E minor pentatonic scale.

Example 32 **Track 43**

Here, we continue working in **7/4** meter, this time using the D minor pentatonic scale: **D-F-G-A-C**.
Pay attention to the tied notes and syncopation that lend interest to this example.

Example 33

Track 44

Here's a new riff in **7/4** time that uses the F♯ minor pentatonic scale: **F♯-A-B-C♯-E**.
Pay attention to the moderately challenging rhythms.

Example 34

Track 45

The following riff is built on the E minor Phrygian scale: **E-F-G-A-B-C-D-E**.
Again, pay attention to the ties.

Example 35

Track 46

In our last example, we use the A minor pentatonic scale over a measure of **9/4 time**.
Remember the specifics given for this meter.

Summary: Using these examples as a model, build phrases in 5/4, 7/4 and 9/4 time; use different rhythm values and incorporate them in your own music.

CHAPTER 3
Exploring Exotic Scales

Although less commonly used in modern music, it's important to pay attention to the world of exotic scales; they offer many creative and experimental options that can enrich our compositions and solos. This chapter will present a brief explanation of the principal exotic scales, their respective digitation, and finally—examples of how to use them in a musical context.

It's important to clarify that the study and analysis of exotic scales is much more complex and involved than represented here, given that each civilization (China, Greece, India, Arabia, Japan, etc.) has developed its own musical system.

THE HIRAJOSHI SCALE

The Hirajoshi scale is a Japanese pentatonic scale obtained by omitting the 4 and ♭7 degrees of the natural minor scale. It works perfectly on the same harmonic principles as the natural minor scale. It has a classic Far Eastern sound due to the existence of two minor second intervals.

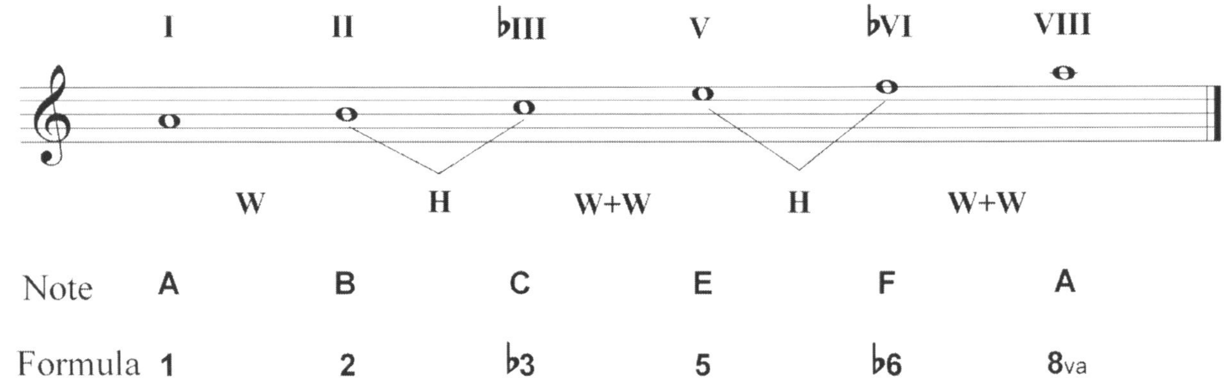

FINGERING OF THE HIRAJOSHI SCALE

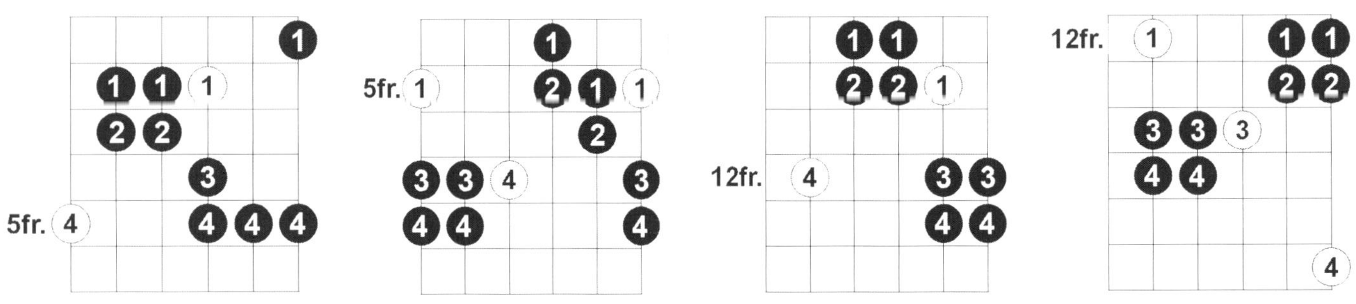

Here are some examples of the application of the Hirajoshi scale:

THE IWATO SCALE

This Japanese pentatonic scale contains the same notes as the Locrian mode except for the ♭3 and ♭6 degrees. It can also be considered as the 2nd mode of the Hirajoshi scale. Lacking its third degree, this scale is best used over a drone bass note of the same name.

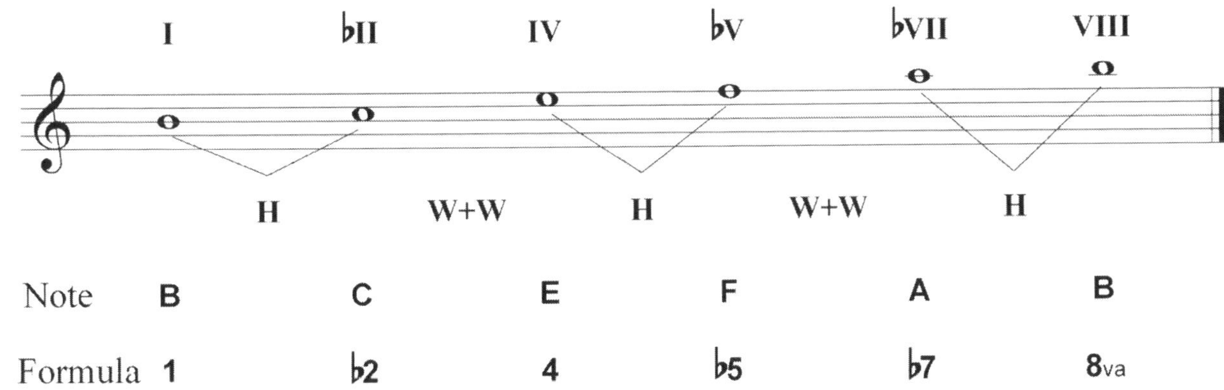

FINGERING OF THE IWATO SCALE

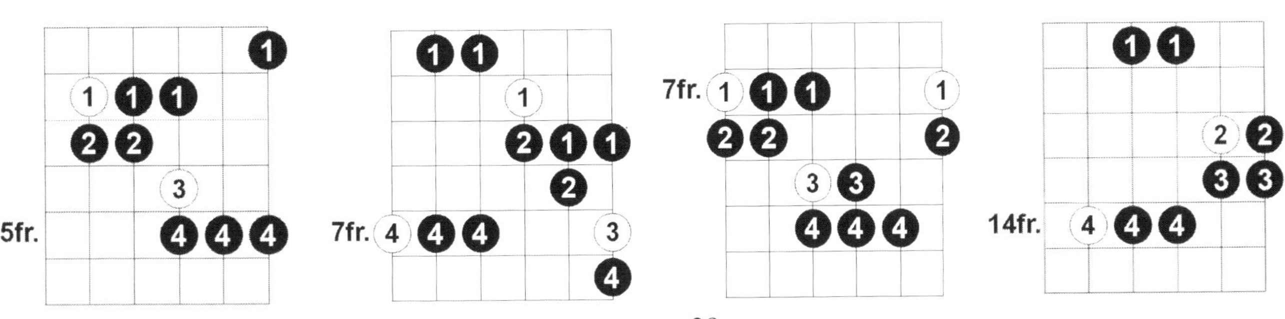

Here are some applications of the Iwato scale:

Example 38

Track 49

Example 39

Track 50

Example 40

Track 51

THE HON KUMOI SCALE

The Hon Kumoi scale is another Japanese pentatonic scale containing the same notes as the Phrygian mode but with the ♭3 and ♭7 degrees omitted. It can also be considered as the 4th mode of the Hirajoshi scale. It can be applied to minor m7 and m6 chords as well as to dominant chords of minor keys since it has two main tensions, a ♭2 and ♭6. **It is important not to confuse the Hon Kumoi with the Kumoi scale** as they are two distinct scales.

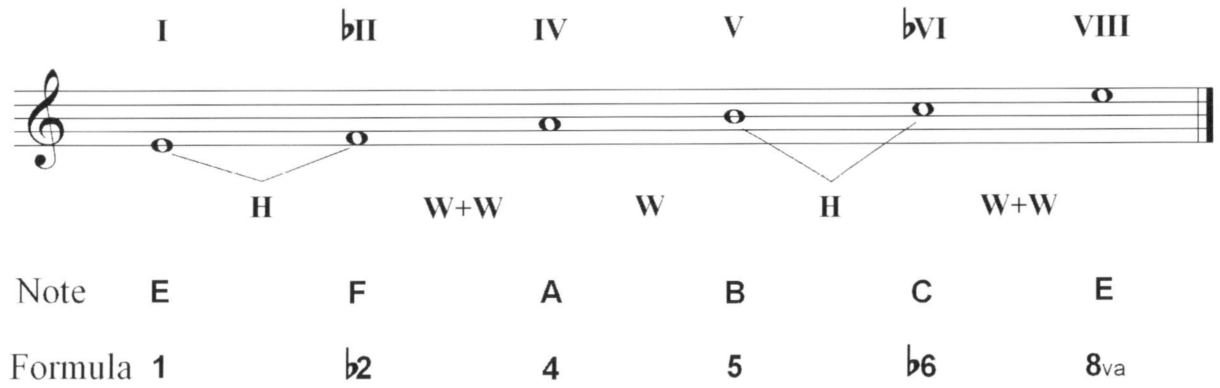

Note	E	F	A	B	C	E
Formula	1	♭2	4	5	♭6	8va

FINGERING OF THE HON KUMOI SCALE

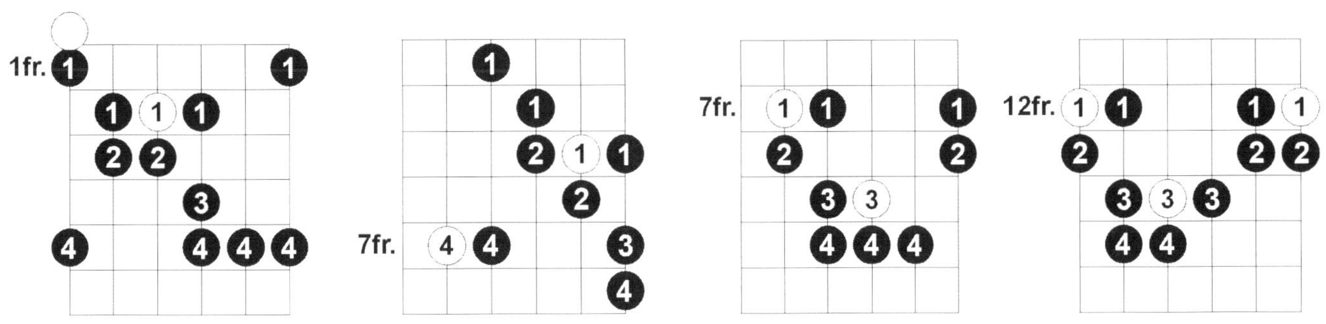

Example 41 **Track 52**

THE KUMOI SCALE

The Kumoi scale is the equivalent of the Dorian mode but without the 4 and ♭7 degrees. It contains a minor third and a major sixth interval. It can be applied to minor chords and minor seventh chords, among others.

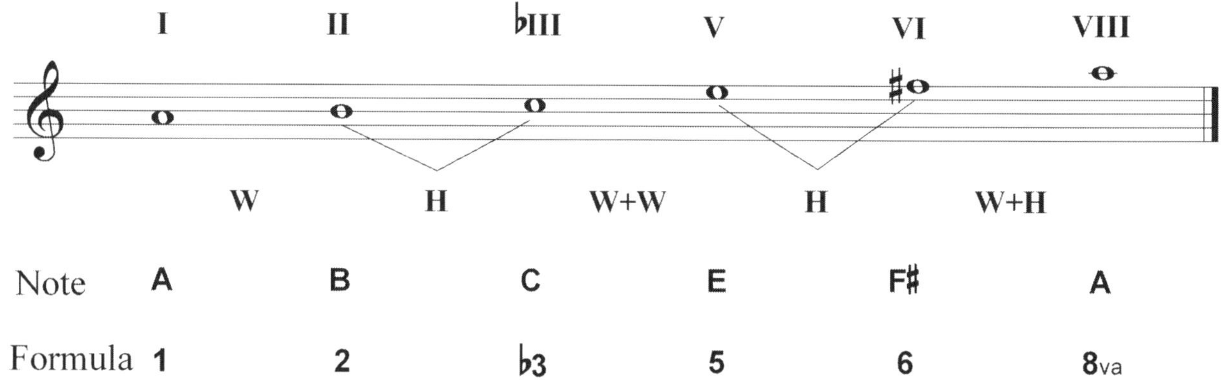

FINGERING OF THE KUMOI SCALE

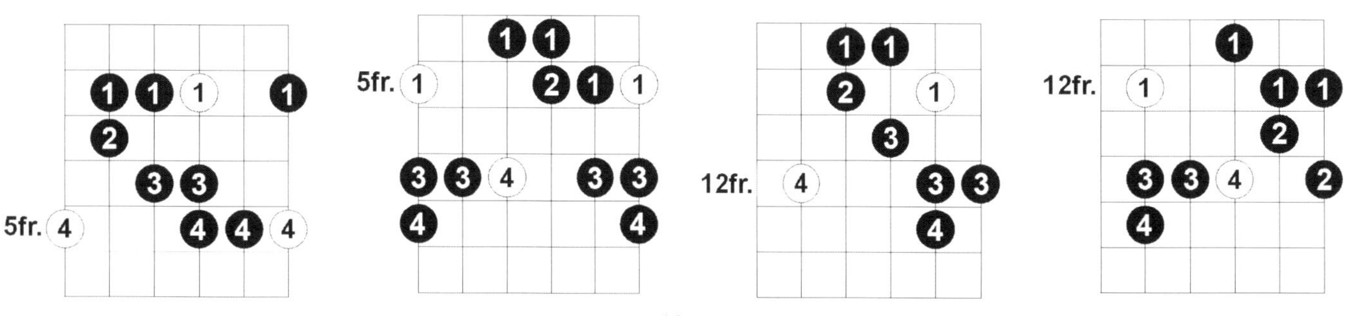

Here are some examples of the application of the Kumoi scale:

Example 44

Track 55

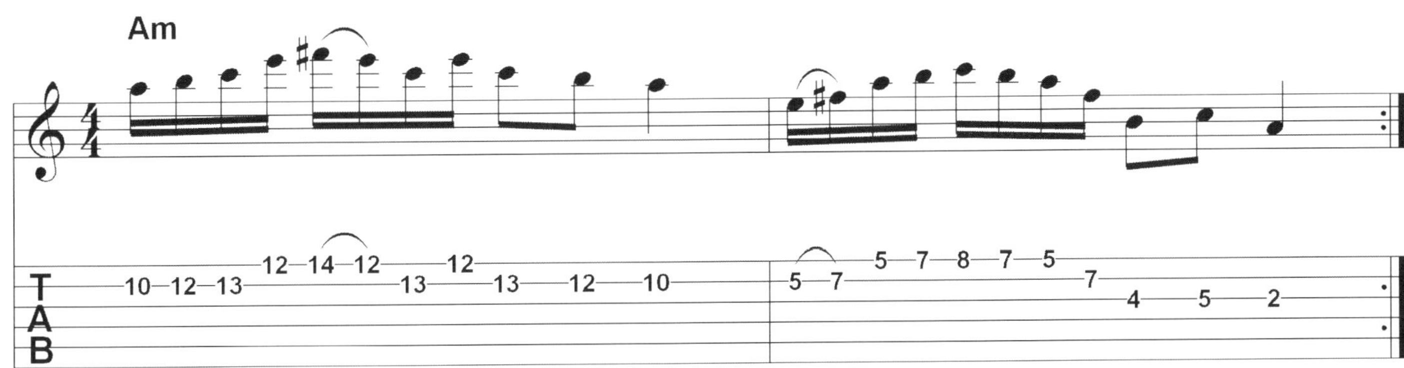

Example 45

Track 56

Example 46

Track 57

THE EGYPTIAN SCALE

This scale is obtained by omitting the ♭3rd and ♭6th degrees of a natural minor scale or the 3rd and 6th degrees of a Mixolydian scale. It can also be considered as the third mode of the minor pentatonic scale; for example, if we play the E minor pentatonic scale **E-G-A-B-D** but starting from the third degree, **A-B-D-E-G,** we would be playing the Egyptian scale.

The Egyptian scale is also called the "suspended pentatonic". It can be applied to sus 4 chords, dominant chords and minor chords since its construction omits the interval of a third.

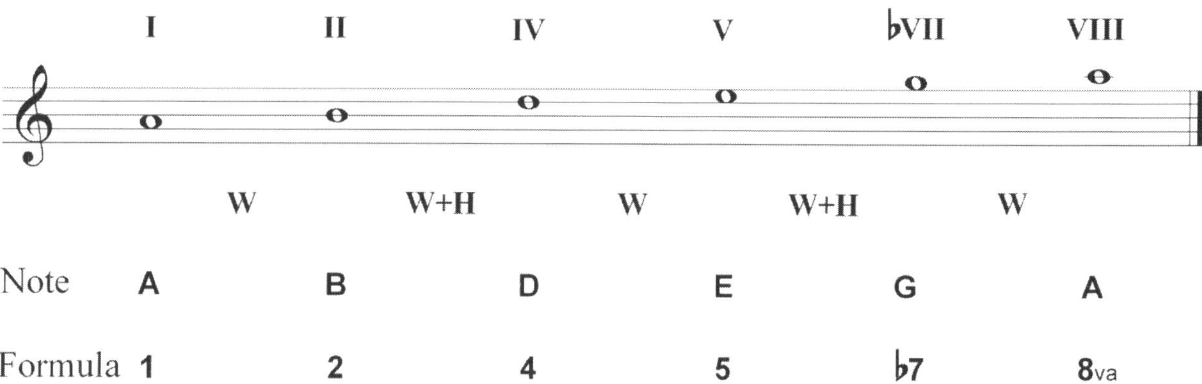

FINGERING THE EGYPTIAN SCALE

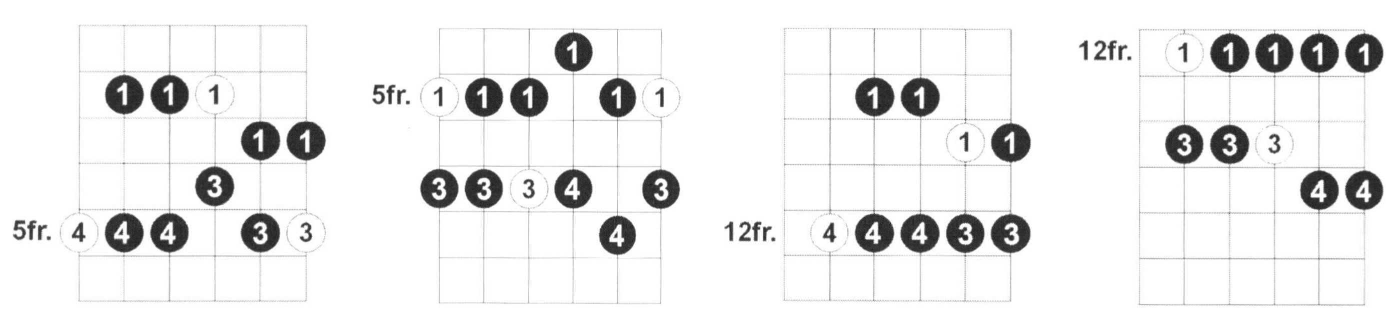

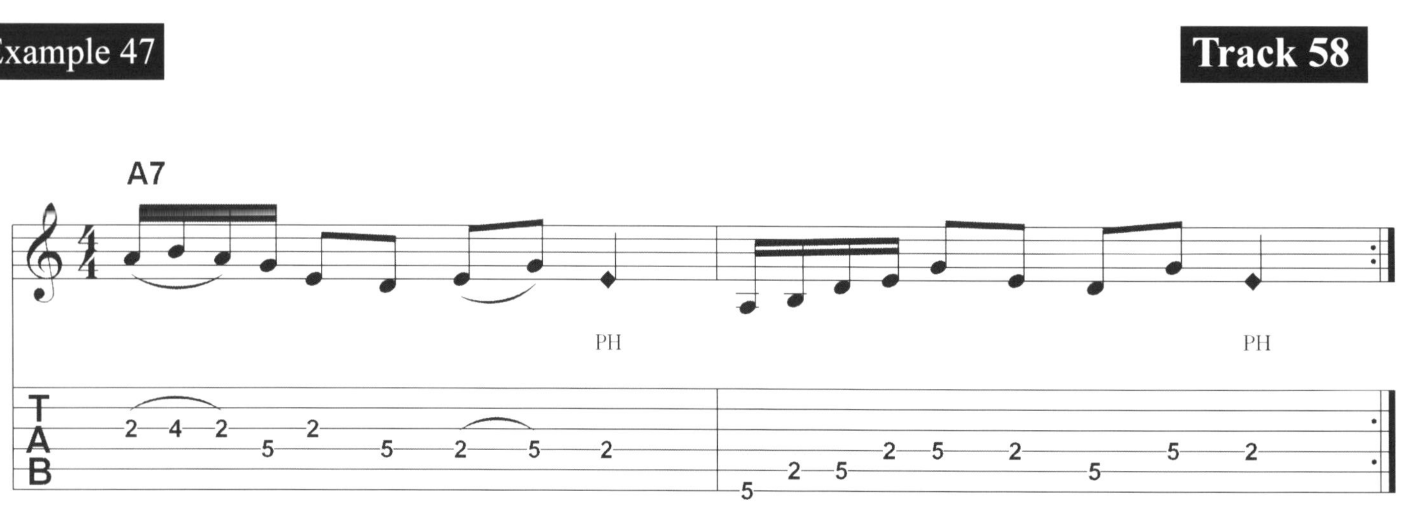

THE RITUSEN SCALE

The Ritusen scale is the fifth mode of the minor pentatonic scale. For example, if we play the B minor pentatonic scale **(B D E F♯ A)** from its fifth mode, we get the Ritusen scale **(A B D E F♯)**. It can be applied on sus chords and on major and minor chords as it omits the interval of a third.

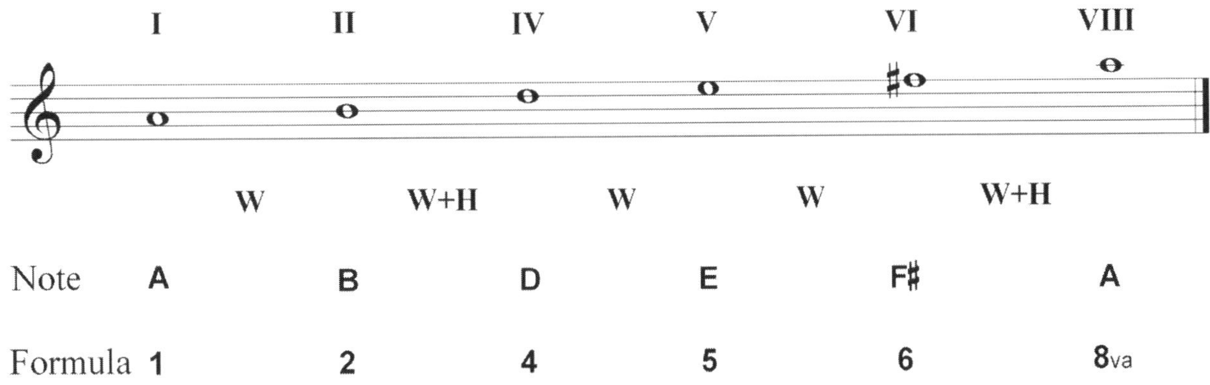

Note	A	B	D	E	F♯	A
Formula	1	2	4	5	6	8va

FINGERING OF THE RITUSEN SCALE

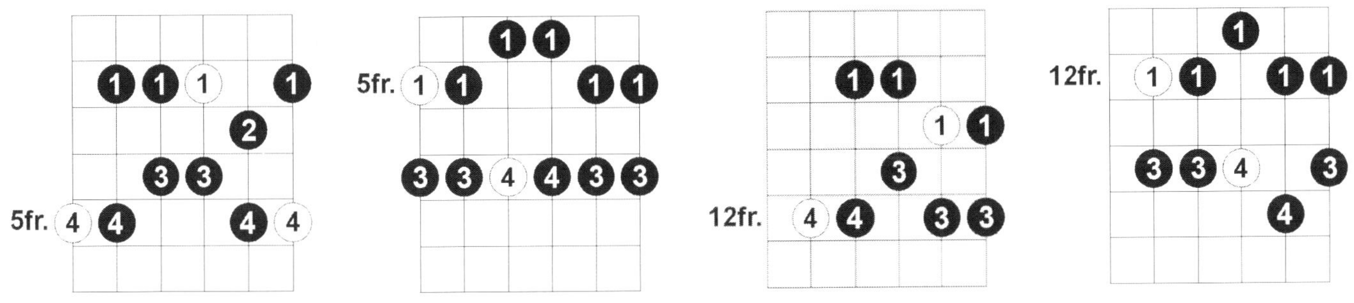

Here is an example of the application of the Ritusen scale:

THE INDIAN SCALE

The Indian scale can be interpreted as a Mixolydian scale with a flat-7 degree: **1-2-3-4-5-6-♭7,** but with the 2nd and 6th degrees omitted **(1-3-4-5-♭7)**. It is usually called a dominant pentatonic or minor pentatonic with its major third. We can also observe that it contains the notes of the dominant 7 arpeggio **(A-C♯-E-G)** plus the perfect fourth. It can be applied over a dominant seventh chord or power chord of the same name.

[For a complete introduction to the 72 scales in the Melakarta Indian system, see Mel Bay's *Elements of Indian Music* (30603M) by Radhika Iyer.]

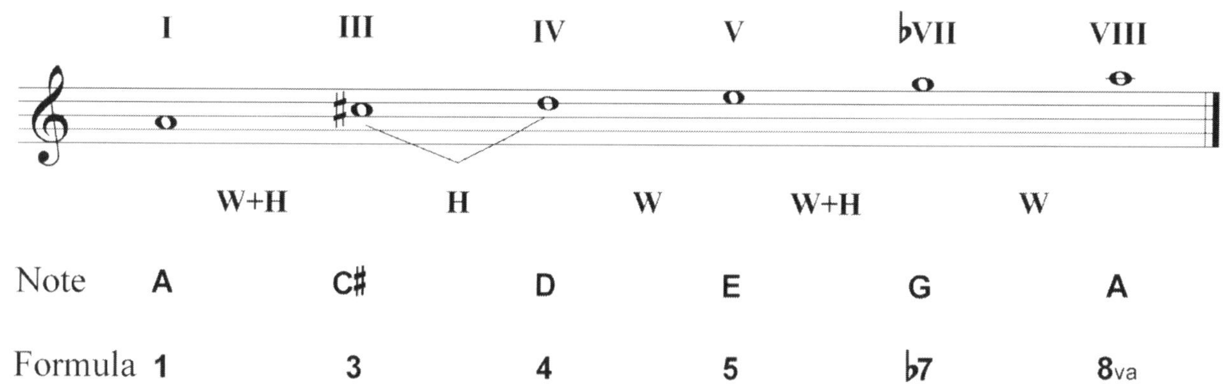

FINGERING OF THE INDIAN SCALE

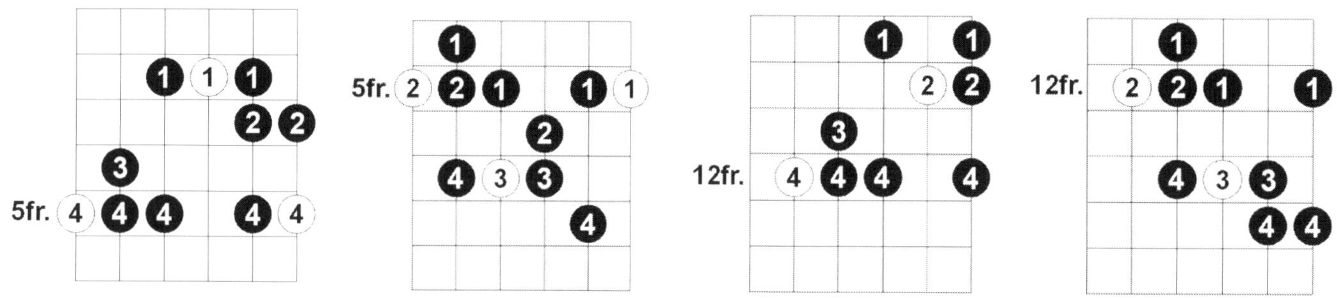

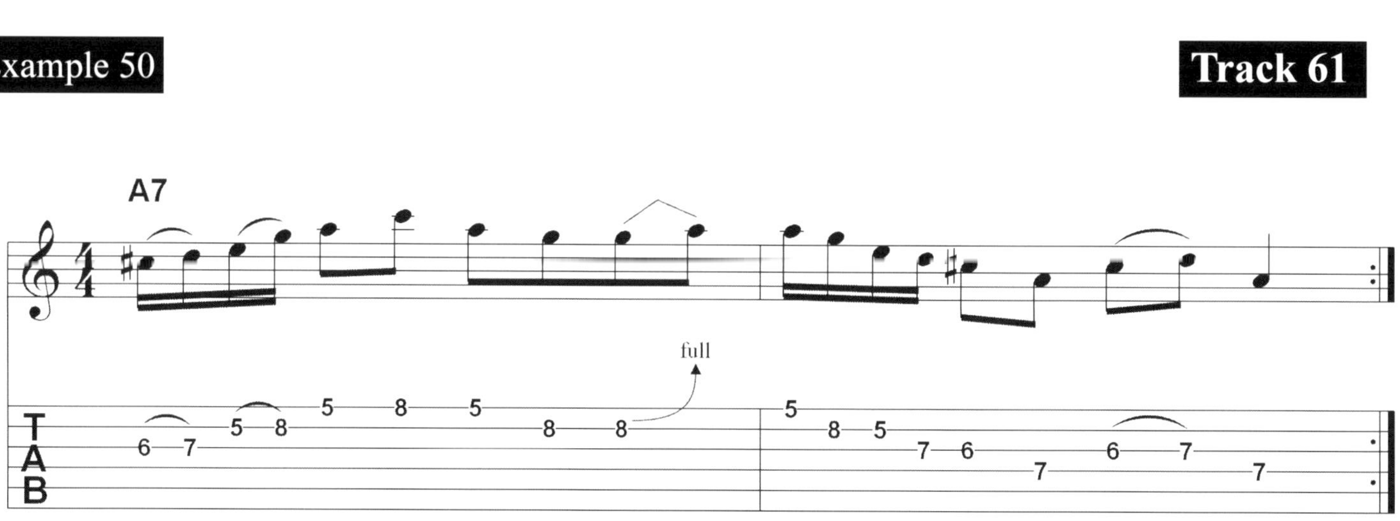

Example 51

Track 62

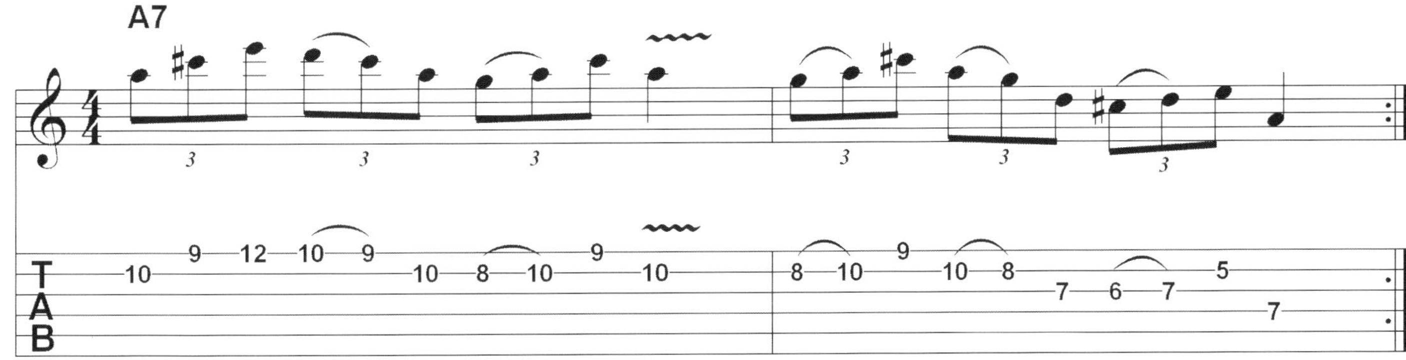

THE CHINESE SCALE

The Chinese scale is used universally, but especially in central Asian countries. Keep in mind that this scale is based on sequential intervals of a perfect fifth **(A E B F♯ C♯)** and that in ancient Chinese culture, the number five had a spiritual connotation. Like Indian scales, there are numerous Chinese scales, but in general, this is the most common one. In Western music this scale is known as the **pentatonic major**. China exerted a great cultural influence on neighboring civilizations in Japan, Korea, Mongolia, etc.—ultimately having an extreme effect on American blues.

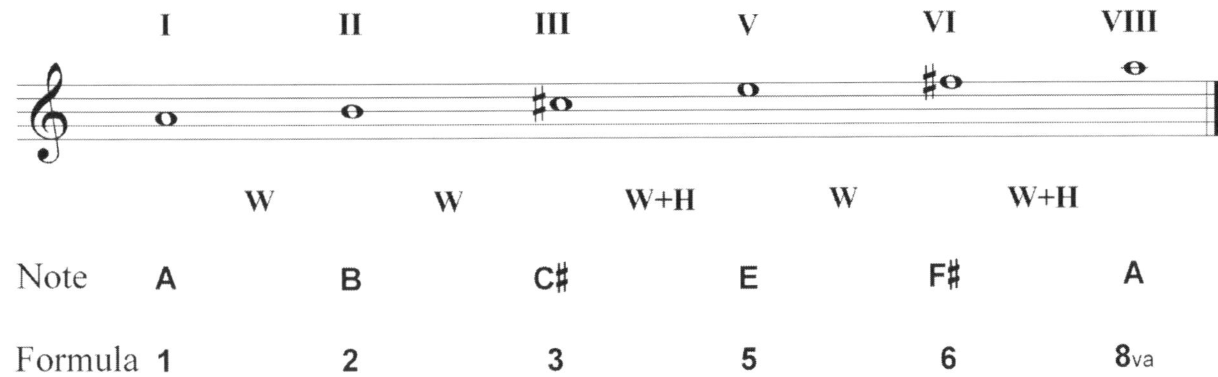

FINGERING OF THE CHINESE SCALE

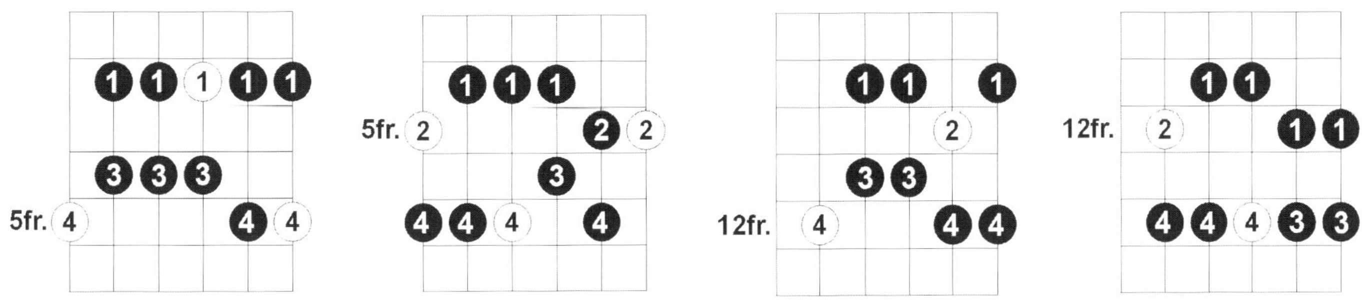

Example 52

Track 63

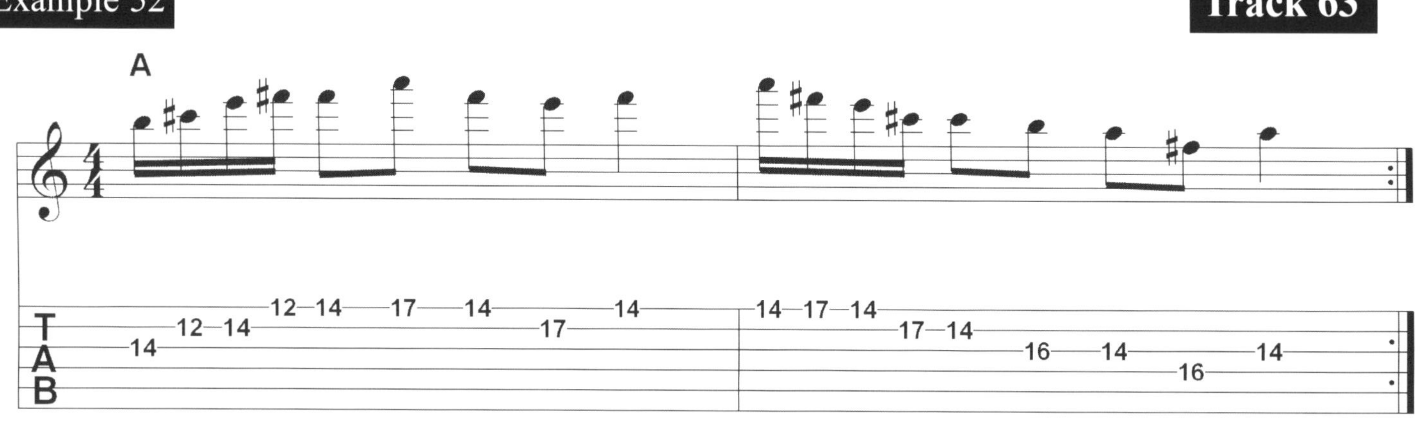

Example 53

Track 64

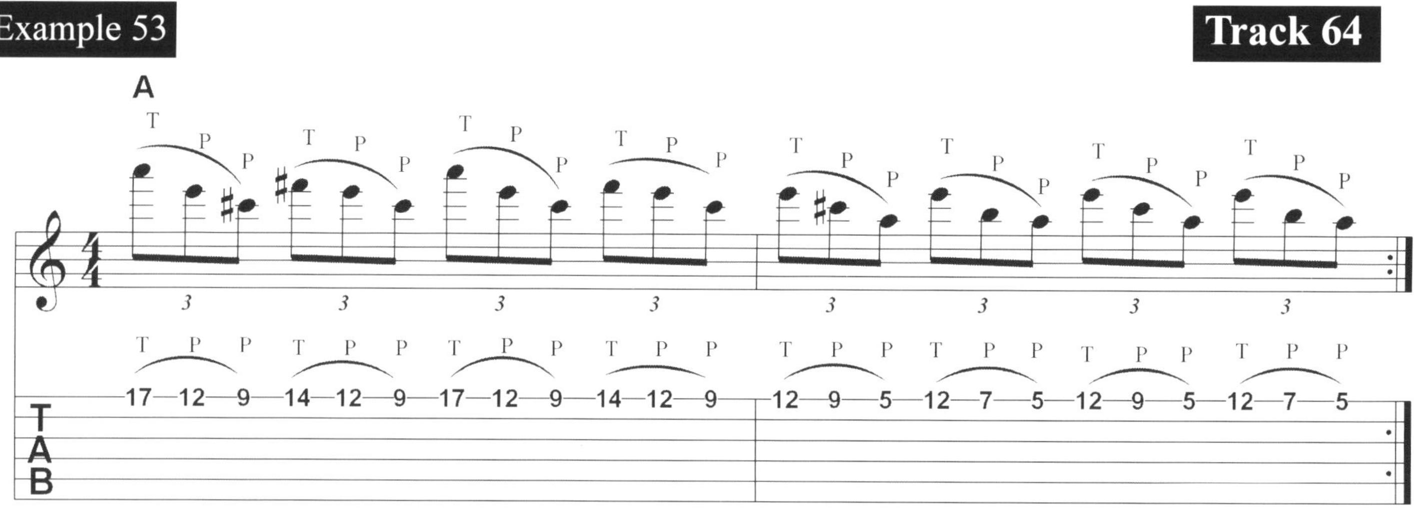

THE PELOG SCALE

The Pelog scale can be interpreted as the Phrygian mode, but with the 4th and flat-7 degrees omitted. This Indonesian scale can be played over the minor triad, m7, m7♭5 and power chords of the same name.

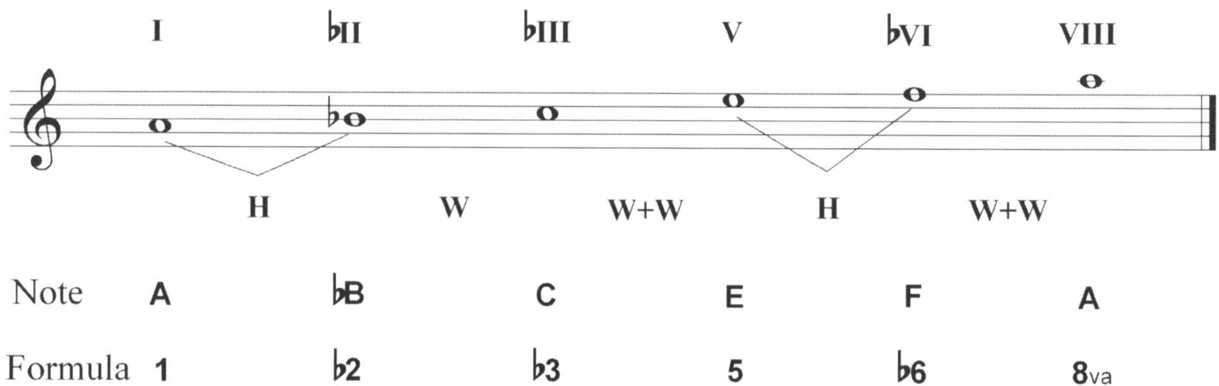

FINGERING OF THE PELOG SCALE

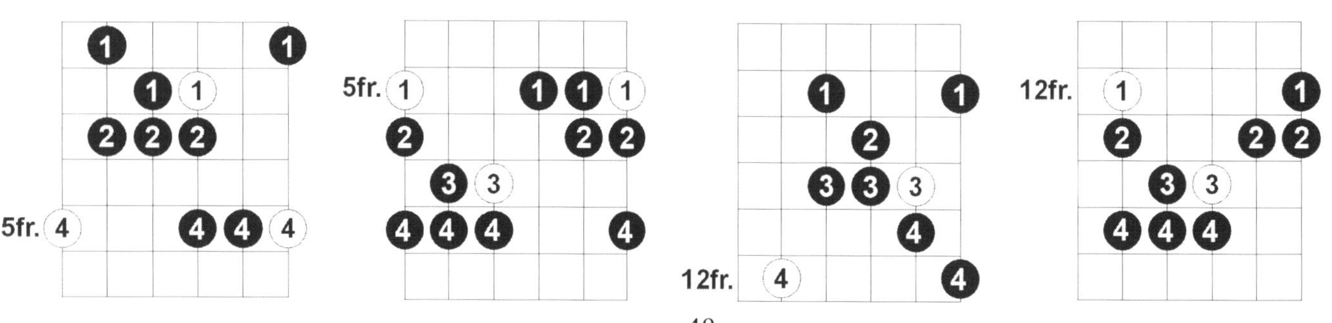

Example 54

Track 65

Example 55

Track 66

Example 56

Track 67

THE BYZANTINE SCALE

This scale is formed by two harmonic tetrachords. Its notes contain a Maj7 chord and two sensitive notes—a lower sensitive (♭2) and an upper sensitive (7) plus two intervals of an augmented second. It's interesting that this scale has the same intervals ascending and descending.

This scale is also known as the **double harmonic major** because of those two harmonic tetrachords, the Gypsy major, the surf rock scale, and the Hungarian major scale. It can be played over a major chord, maj7 or power chord of the same name.

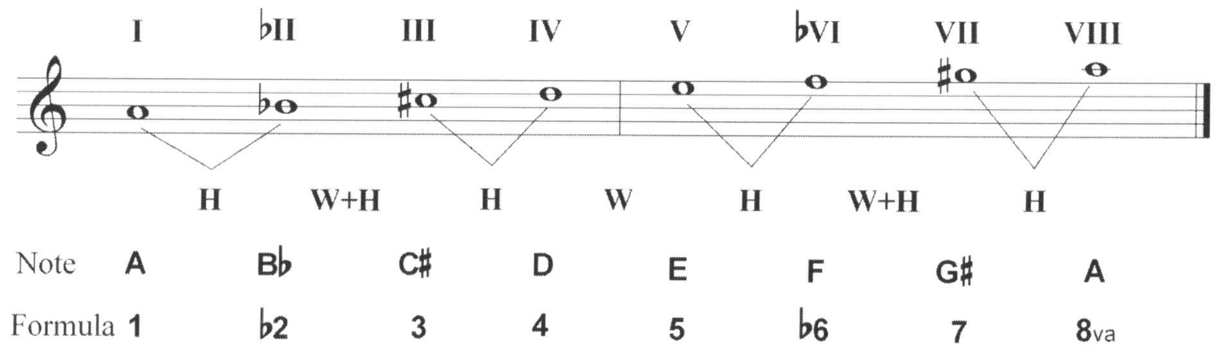

FINGERING OF THE BYZANTINE SCALE

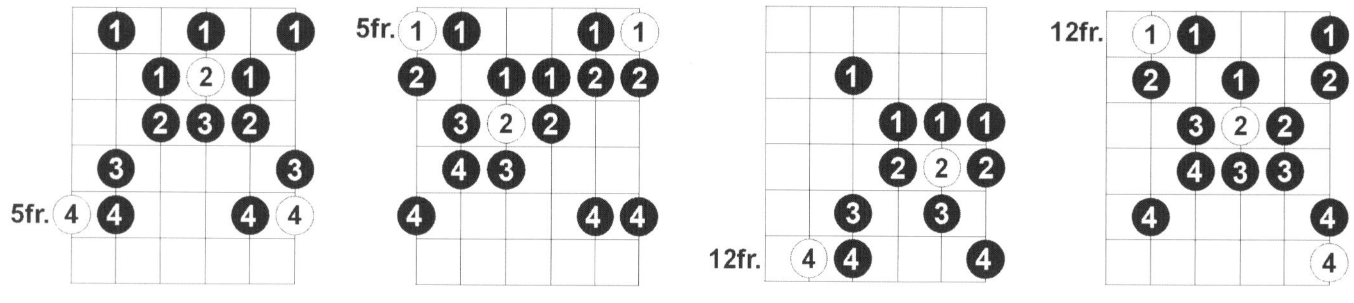

Example 57

Track 68

Example 58 **Track 69**

CREATING NEW ARTIFICIAL SCALES FROM THE HARMONIC MINOR SCALE

The interval of an augmented second (W+H) located between the 6th and 7th degrees of the harmonic minor scale gives rise to a unique upper tetrachord. This interval can be displaced by changing the starting point of the scale to another degree of the harmonic minor scale, generating new harmonic tetrachords. Let's examine the tetrachords in the normal A harmonic minor scale, and then the changes made in the position of the augmented second interval in the upper tetrachord by starting on degrees II and VII of the same scale.

A. In the first example, we see the augmented second in its usual position between VI and VII in the normal A harmonic minor scale:

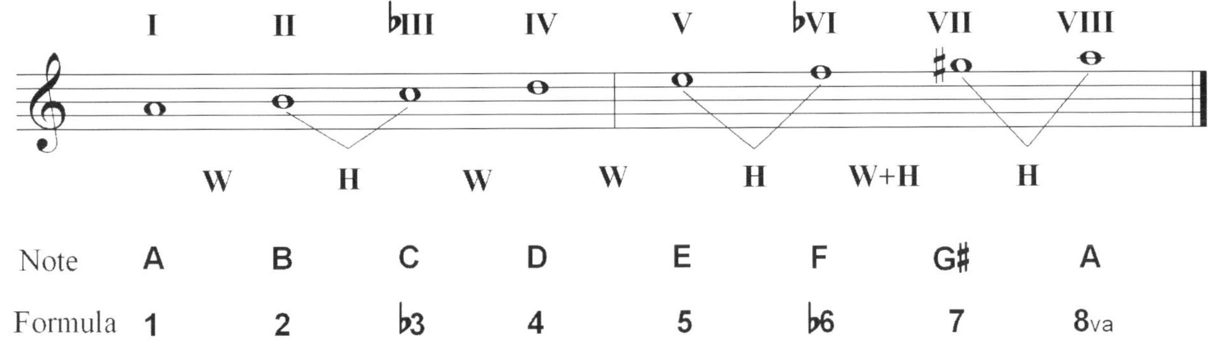

B. Now, starting on B—the augmented second interval is relocated between degrees V and VI.

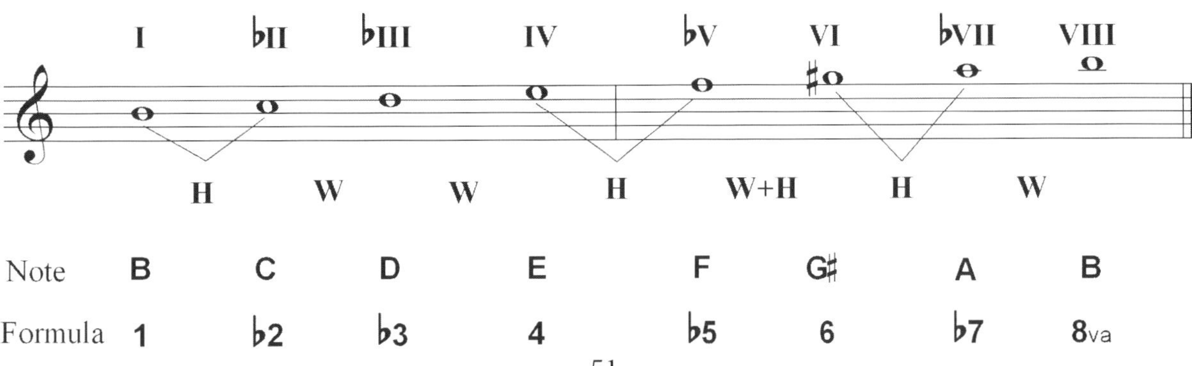

C. Finally, if we start from the VII degree of the A harmonic minor scale (G♯), the augmented second interval occurs between degrees VII and VIII.

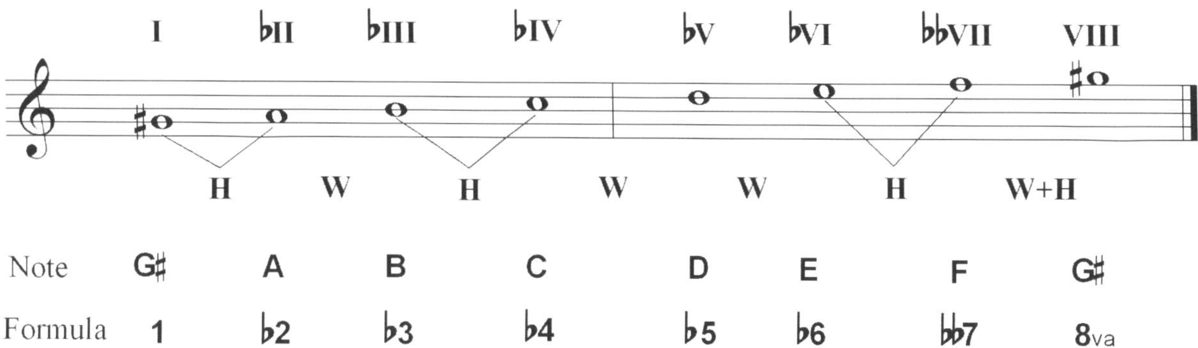

In summary, changing the starting point of the scale from I (A) to II (B) and VII (G♯) of the A harmonic minor scale creates upper Harmonic Tetrachords 2 and 3 below:

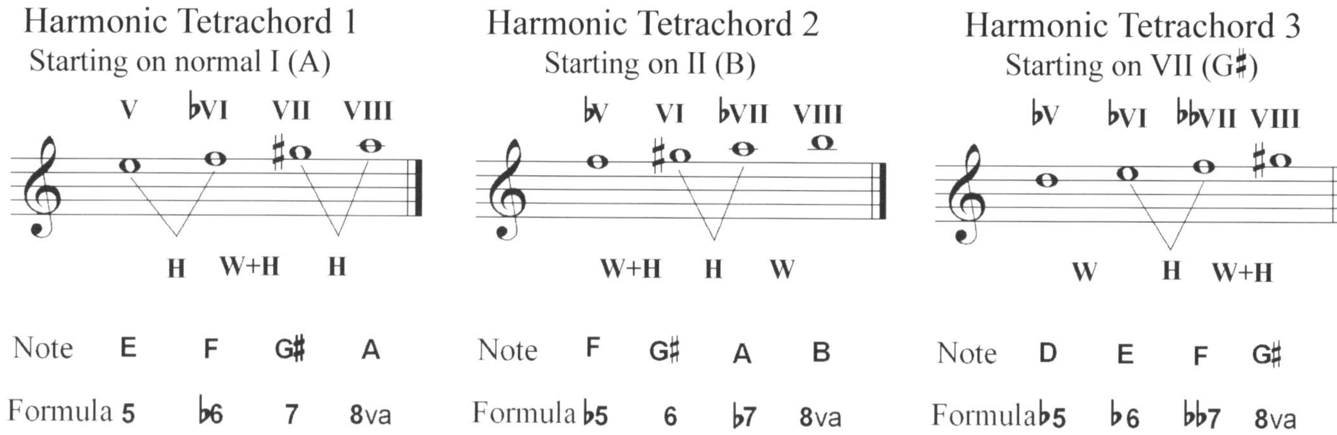

Artificial scales contain altered tones and as a result they do not have their own key signatures. Major scales, pure minor scales and the modal scales built from major scales are all "naturally occurring" scales; by contrast, harmonic and melodic minor scales are already "artificial" in that they contain altered tones.
By relocating the tonic within the already artificial harmonic minor scale, and futher displacing the whole tones, half tones and augmented second interval, we are creating still more artificial scales.

The combination of these tetrachords with each other or with other modal tetrachords results in a whole new range of artificial scales and soloing possibilities!

THE HUNGARIAN MINOR SCALE

This scale is the fourth mode of the Byzantine scale. In other words, we play the Byzantine scale **(A-B♭-C♯-D-E-F-G♯-A)** but start from its fourth degree **(D-E-F-G♯-A-B♭-C♯).**

Other names for this scale include Algerian, double-harmonic minor, and Gypsy minor.

The Hungarian minor scale can be applied on minor chords, minor/Maj7 or power chords of the same name.

This scale consists of harmonic tetrachord 3 and harmonic tetrachord 1.

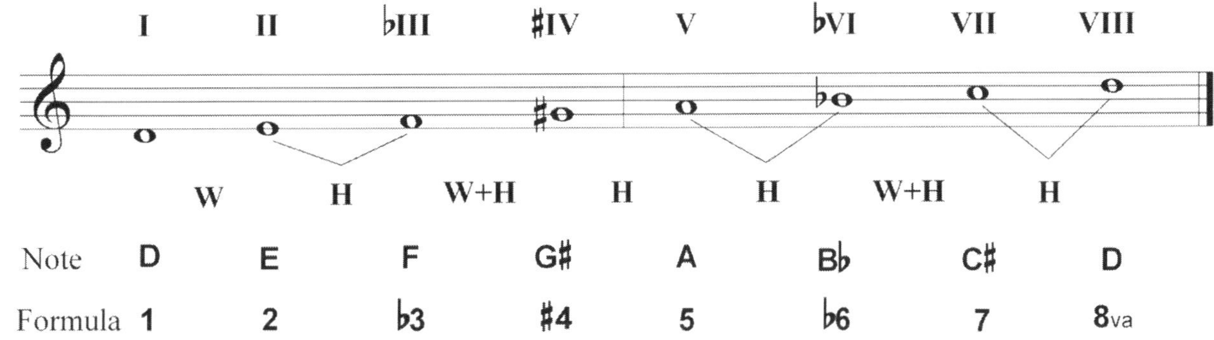

FINGERING OF THE HUNGARIAN MINOR SCALE

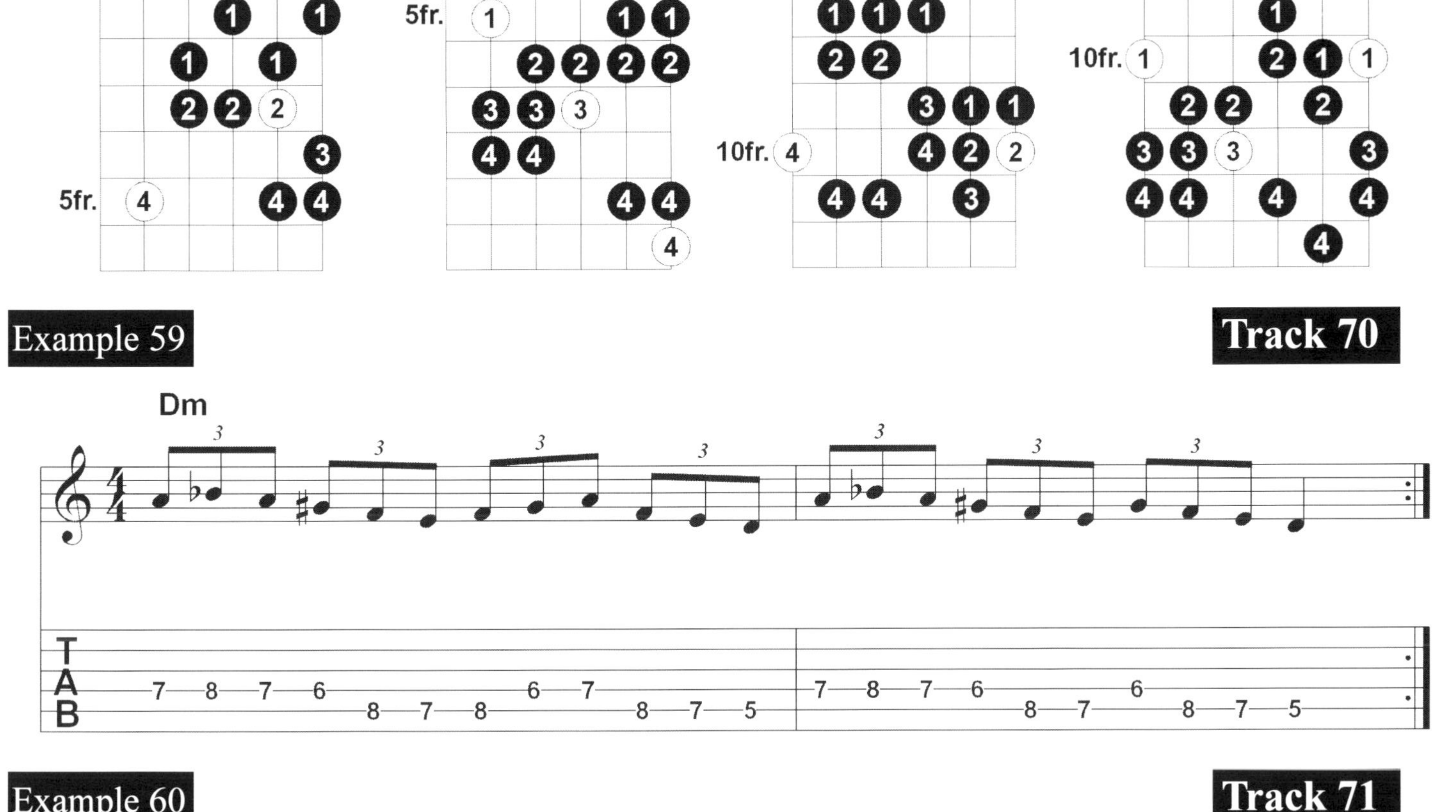

Example 60

Track 71

THE ORIENTAL SCALE

This scale is built from the fifth mode of the Byzantine scale. If we play the Byzantine scale **(A-B♭-C♯-D-E-F-G♯-A)** starting from its fifth degree, we get the Oriental scale: **(E-F-G♯-A-B♭-C♯-D-E)**.
It can be played on a 7♭5, 7 "alt" or power chord of the same name.

The oriental scale is formed by harmonic tetrachord 1 and harmonic tetrachord 2.

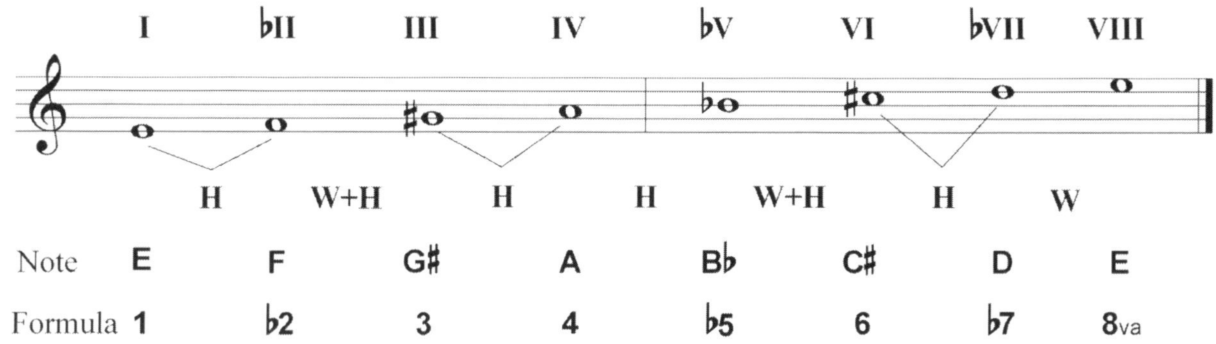

FINGERING OF THE ORIENTAL SCALE

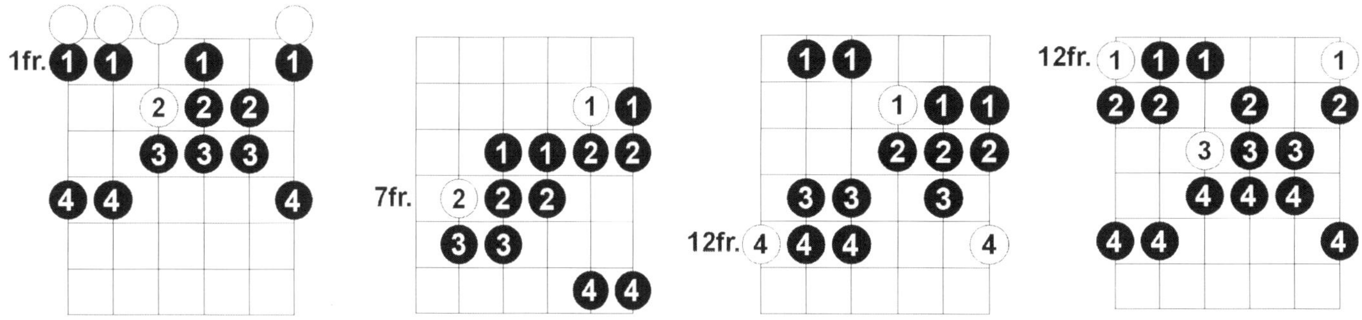

1fr.

7fr.

12fr.

12fr.

Example 61 **Track 72**

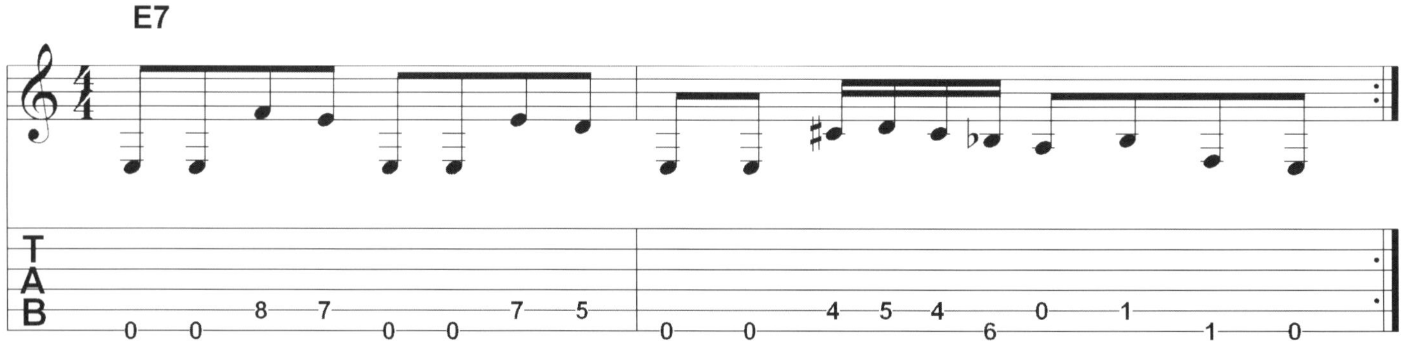

E7

Example 62 **Track 73**

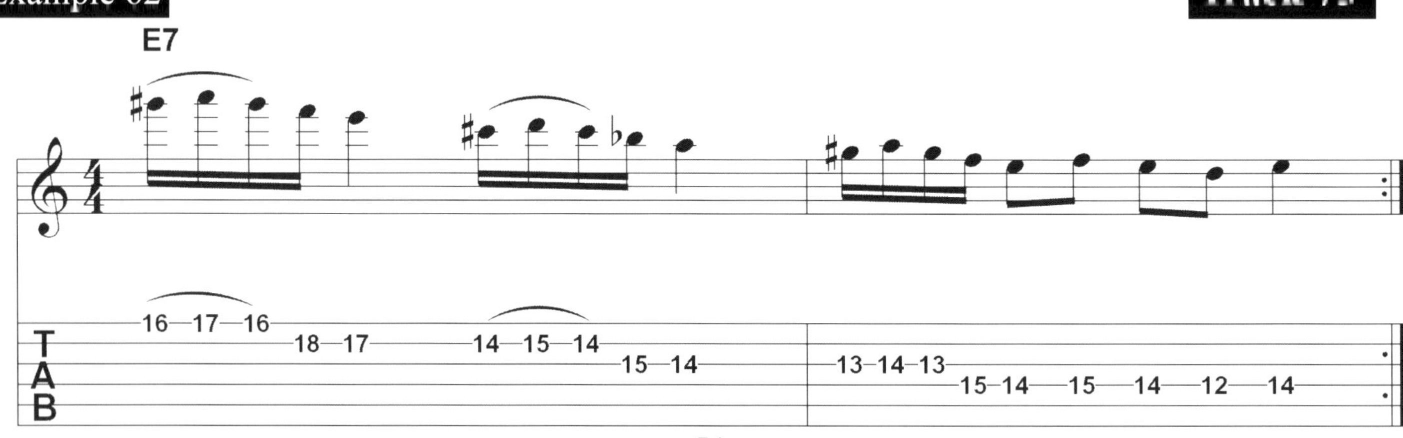

THE GYPSY HUNGARIAN MINOR SCALE

The Gypsy Hungarian minor scale is like the Hungarian minor scale except for its seventh degree, which in this case—is minor.
This scale can be applied over a minor chord, minor seventh or power chord of the same name.

This scale is formed by combining harmonic tetrachord 3 and a Phrygian tetrachord.

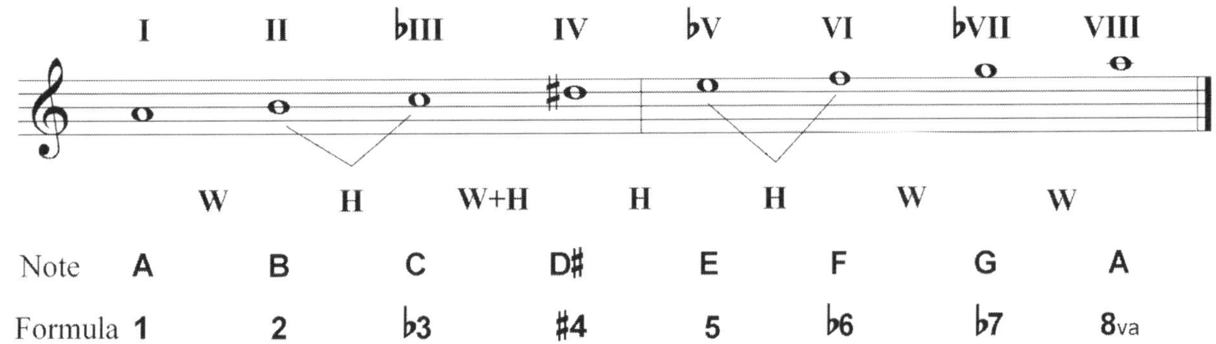

FINGERING OF THE HUNGARIAN MINOR SCALE

5fr.

5fr.

12fr.

12fr.

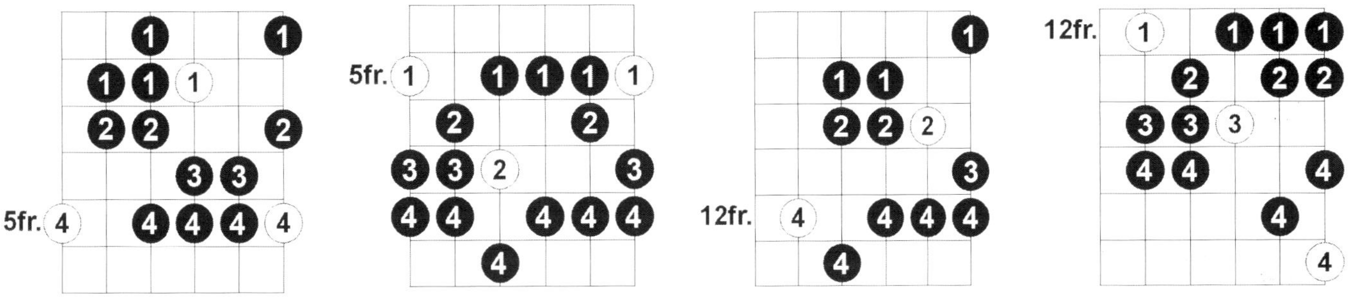

Example 63

Track 74

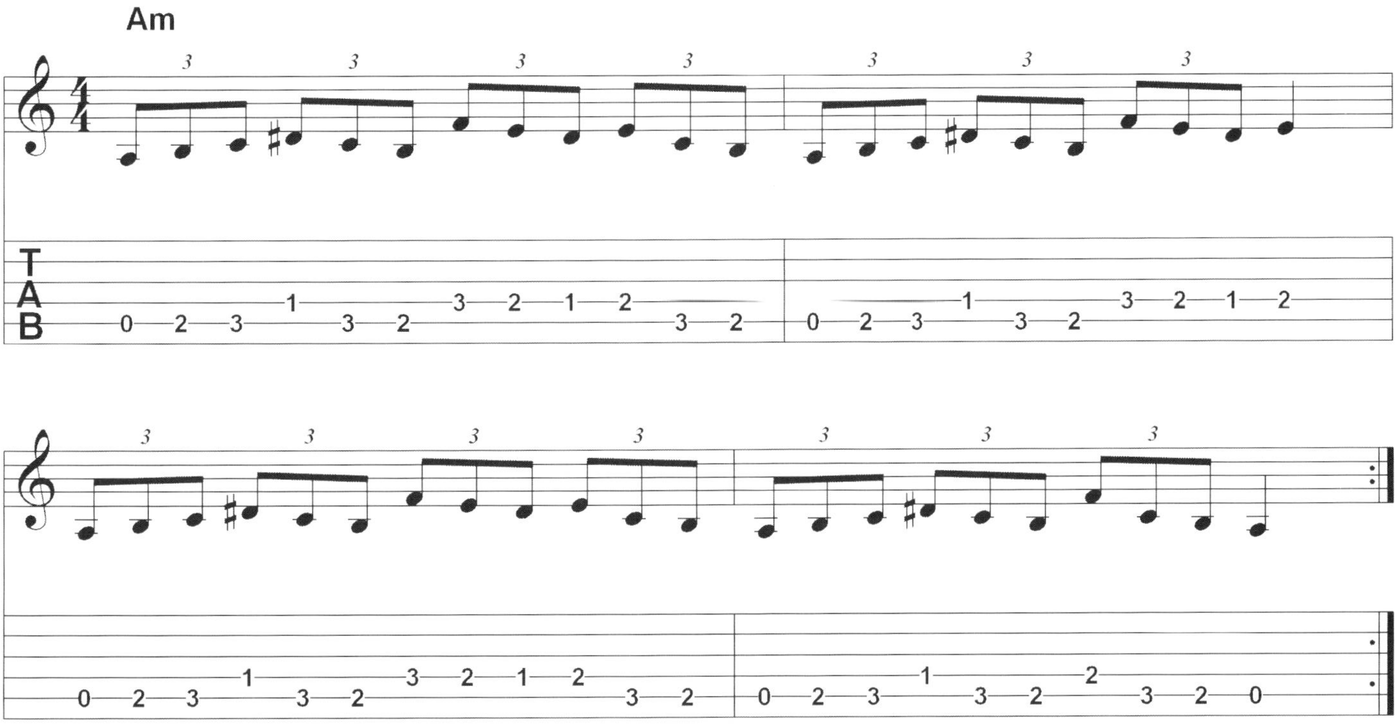

Am

Example 64 Track 75

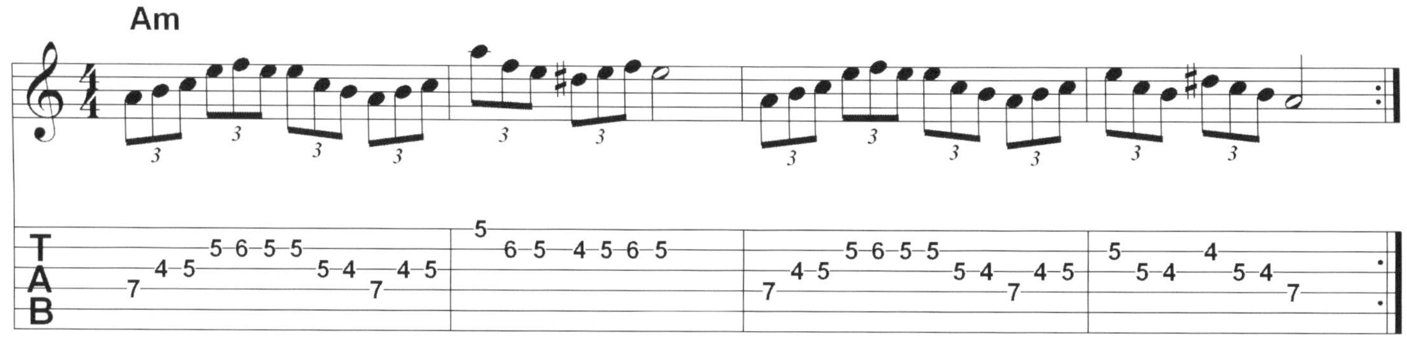

THE PERSIAN SCALE

Inspired by Middle Eastern music, this scale is characterized by its 4 half steps resulting in frequent chromaticism. This scale is formed by two harmonic tetrachords. Notice that it is identical to the Byzantine scale except for its diminished fifth. It can be applied to maj7 chords, (♭5) or power chords of the same name.

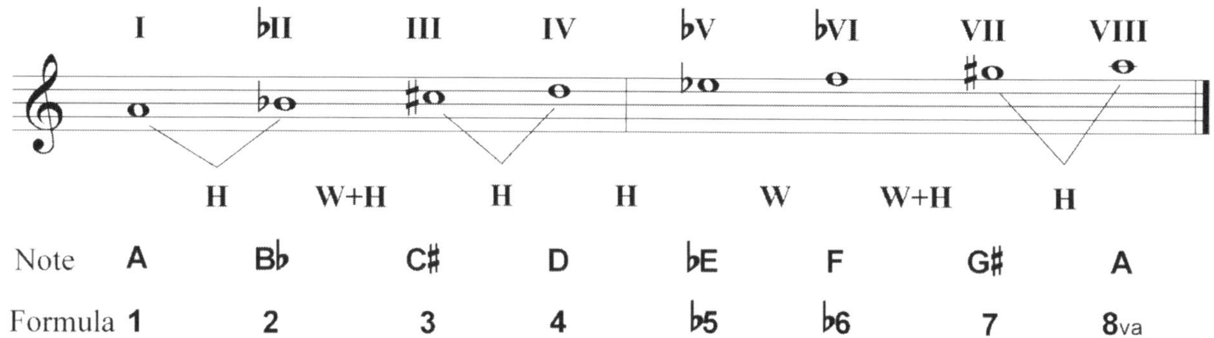

FINGERING OF THE PERSIAN SCALE

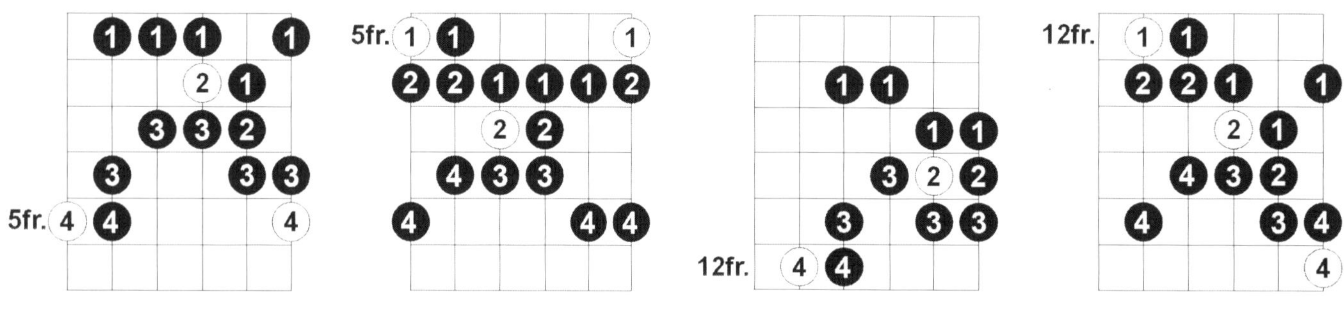

Example 65 Track 76

THE NEAPOLITAN MINOR SCALE

The Neapolitan minor scale is similar to the harmonic minor scale except for its minor second. It can be interpreted as a harmonic minor scale but with a minor second interval at the beginning.
It can be applied over a minor chord, minor ♭6 or minor/maj7 chord.

This scale is formed by the Phrygian tetrachord and harmonic tetrachord 1.

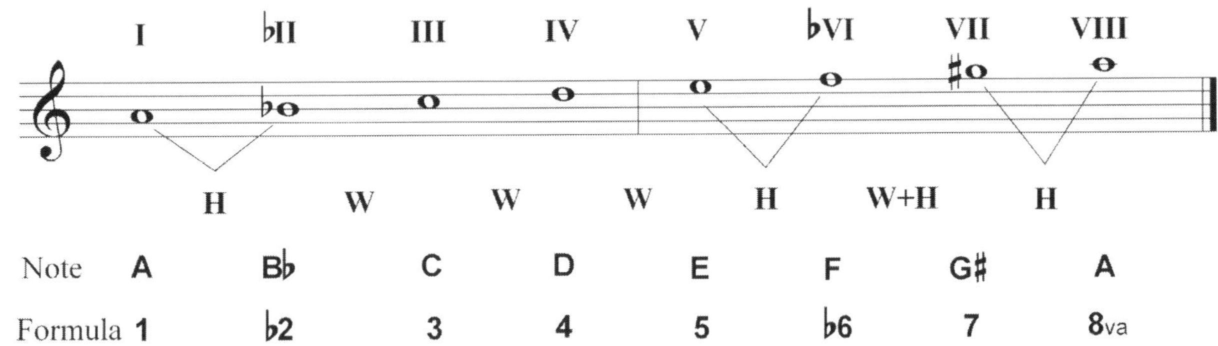

FINGERING OF THE NEAPOLITAN MINOR SCALE

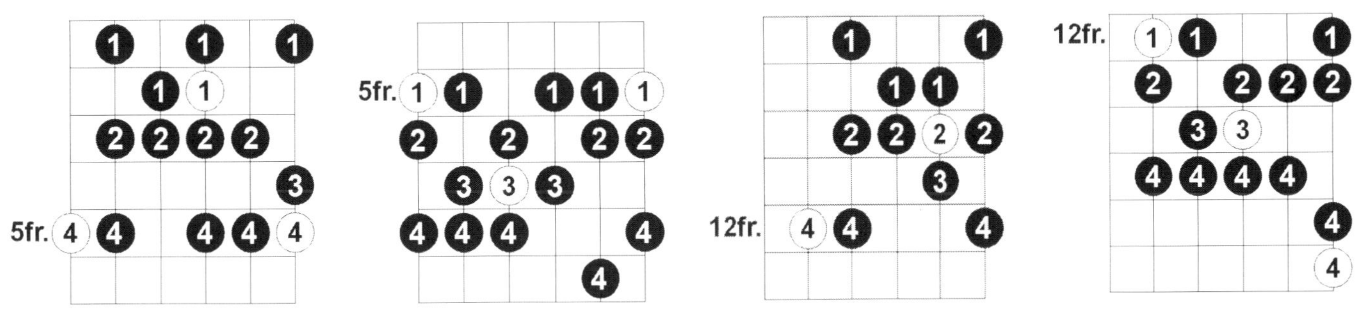

Example 66

Track 77

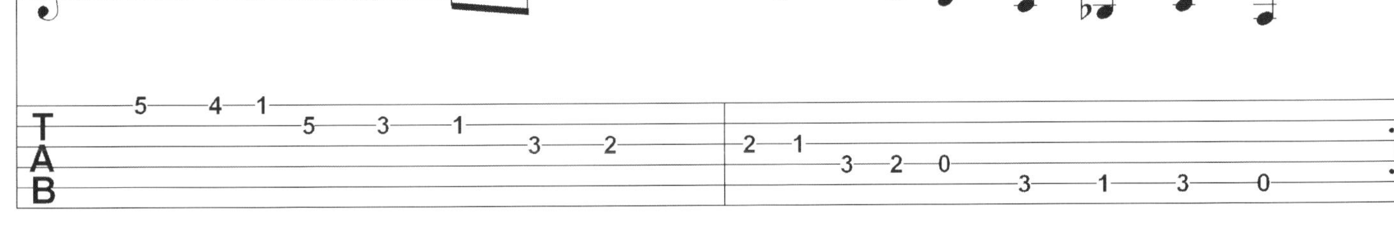

Example 67

Track 78

THE ENIGMATIC SCALE

The enigmatic scale is characterized by a minor second interval at both the low and high ends. It lacks the fourth and perfect fifth intervals which, together with the tonic, are the pillars of tonal music. That's why it is regarded as *enigmatic*. We can also observe 3 consecutive half-step intervals.

The mid-19th century Italian composer Giuseppe Verdi used the enigmatic scale in some of his compositions. There are other forms of the enigmatic scale, but this one is the most common and most often explored in progressive rock soloing. The enigmatic scale can be applied to augmented chords and altered dominants.

FINGERING OF THE ENIGMATIC SCALE

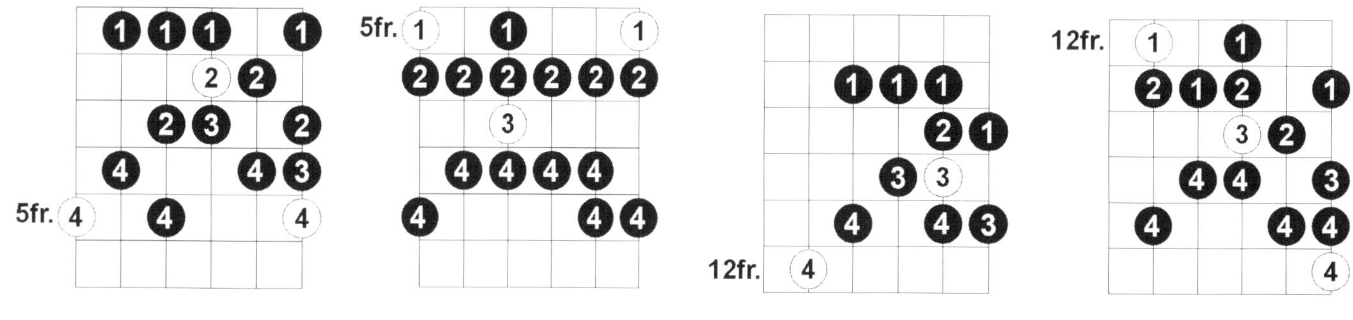

THE PROMETHEUS SCALE

Russian composer Alexander Scriabin (1872-1915) used this hexatonic (6-tone) scale in his work, "Prometheus, the Poem of Fire". For this reason, it is has become known as "The Prometheus Scale". This scale is similar to the Lydian ♭7 mode, except for its perfect fifth. We can also see it as a 6-tone chord, that is, a dominant seventh chord with a diminished fifth (♭5) with 9th and 13th extensions. Scriabin called it "The Mystic Chord".

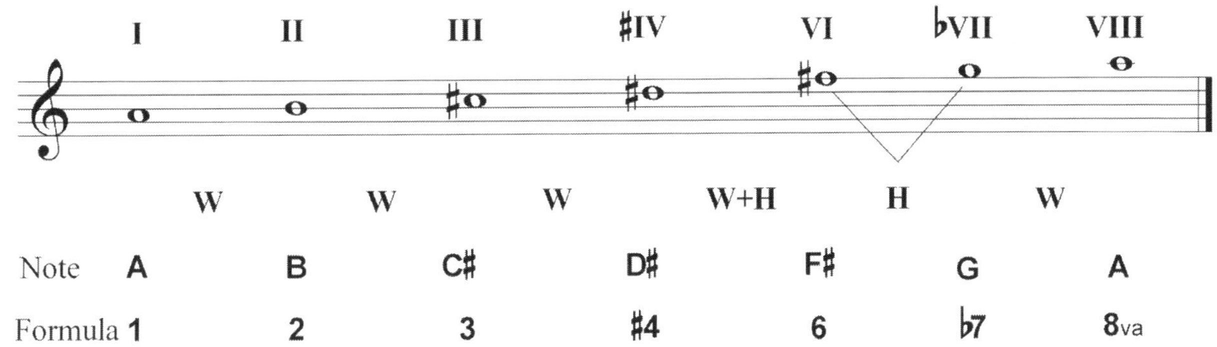

FINGERING OF THE PROMETHEUS SCALE

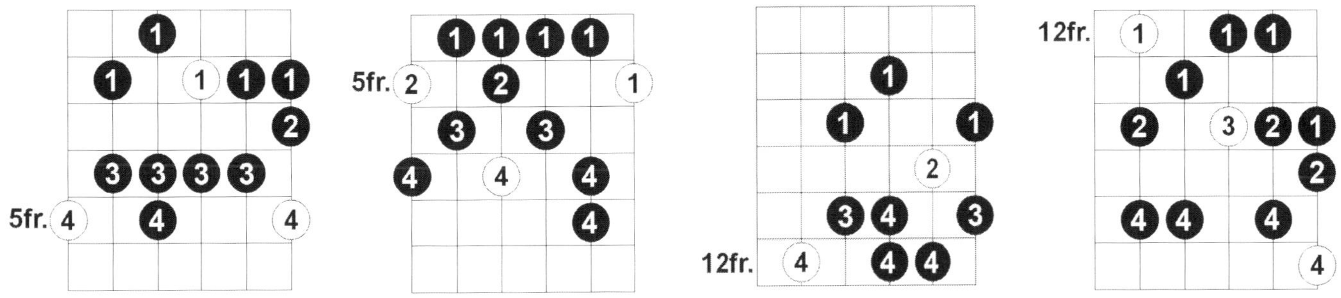

5fr.

5fr.

12fr.

12fr.

Example 70 **Track 81**

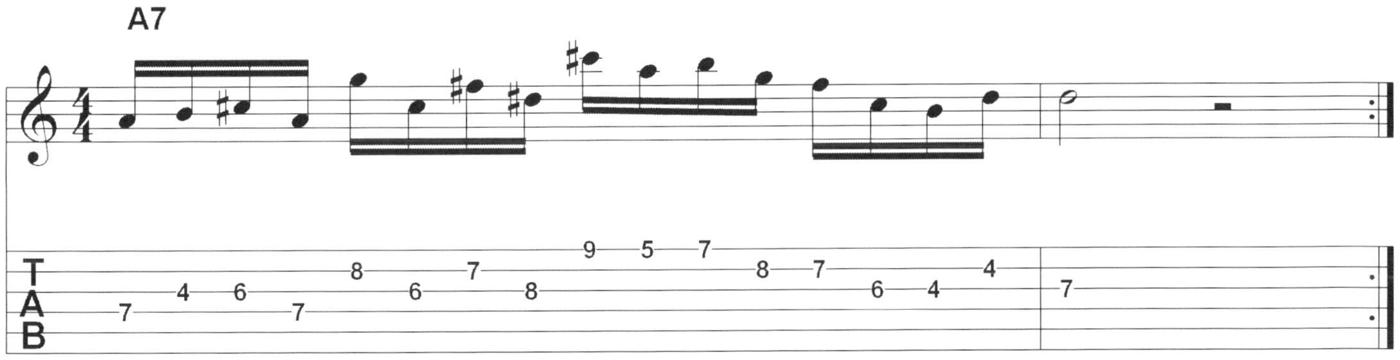

A7

Example 71 **Track 82**

THE PHRYGIAN DOMINANT SCALE

The Phrygian dominant scale is the fifth mode of the harmonic minor scale; in other words, we play the harmonic minor scale **(A-B-C-D-E-F-G♯-A)** but starting from its fifth degree **(E-F-G♯-A-B-C-D-E)**. Its notes exhibit a dominant seventh chord **(E-G♯-B-D)** plus two tensions which are the flat-ninth and the augmented fifth.

This scale is formed by the harmonic tetrachord 1 and the Phrygian tetrachord.

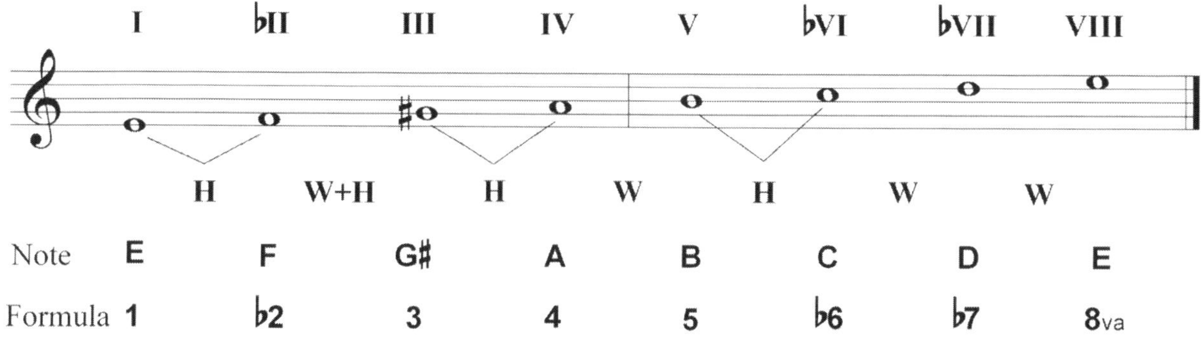

FINGERING OF THE PHRYGIAN DOMINANT SCALE

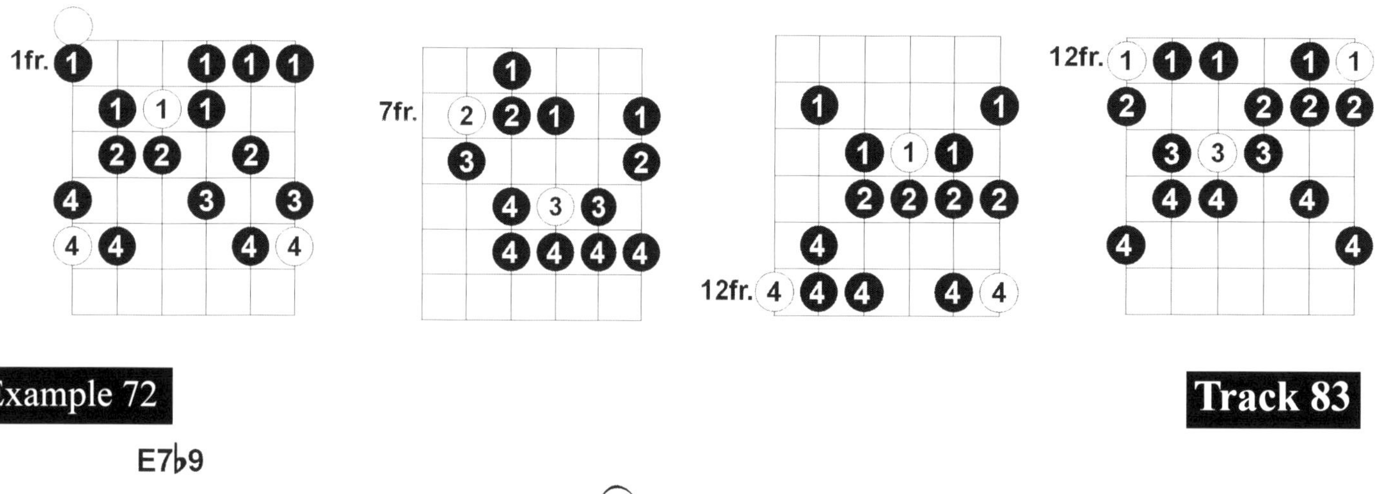

Example 72 **Track 83**

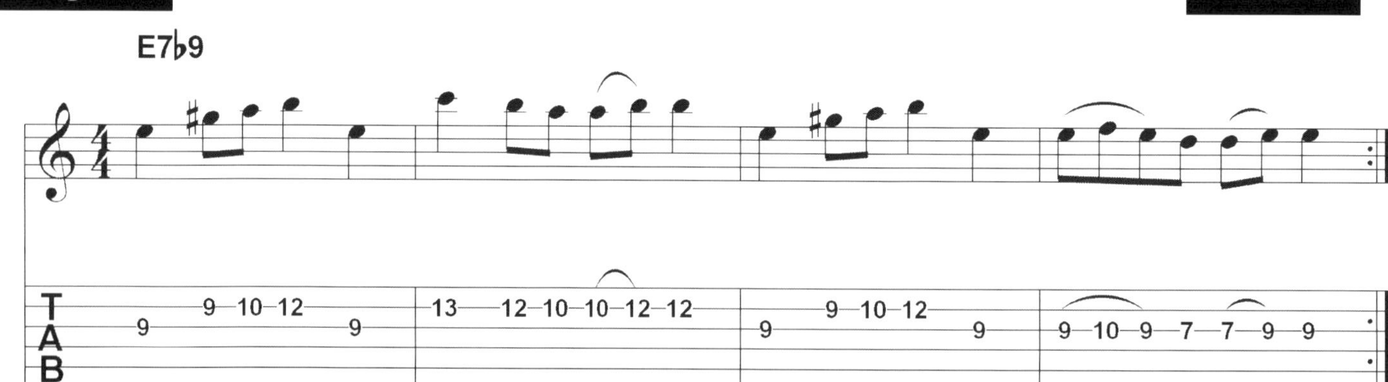

Example 73 **Track 84**

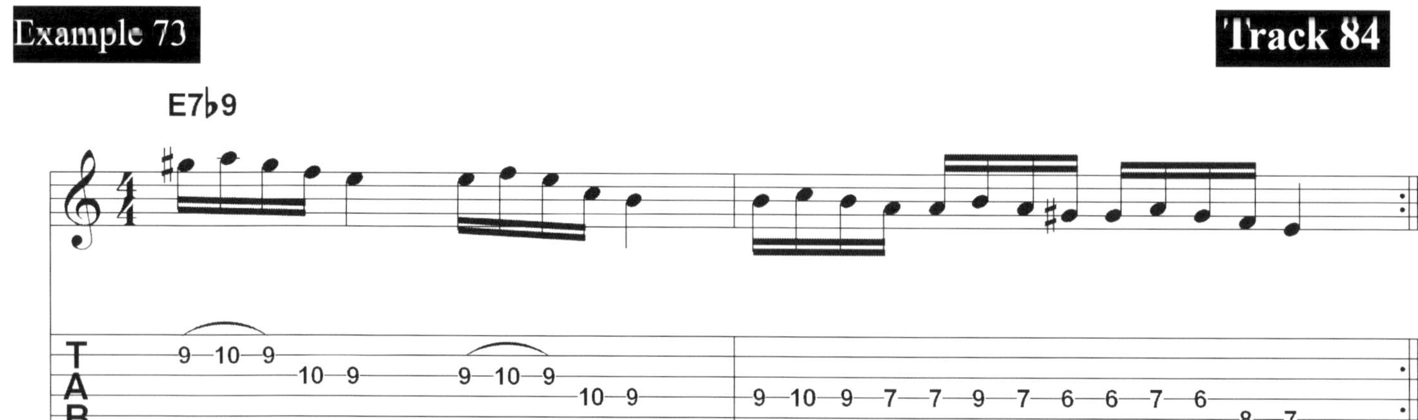

THE HINDU SCALE

The Hindu scale is the fifth mode of the melodic minor scale; that is, we play the melodic minor scale **(A-B-C-D-E-F♯-G♯-A)** starting from its fifth degree **(E-F♯-G♯-A-B-C-D-E)**. Its notes reveal a dominant seventh chord **(E-G♯-B-D)** and the extensions 9, 11 and, as a tension—the minor sixth.

This scale is formed by a major tetrachord and a Phrygian tetrachord.

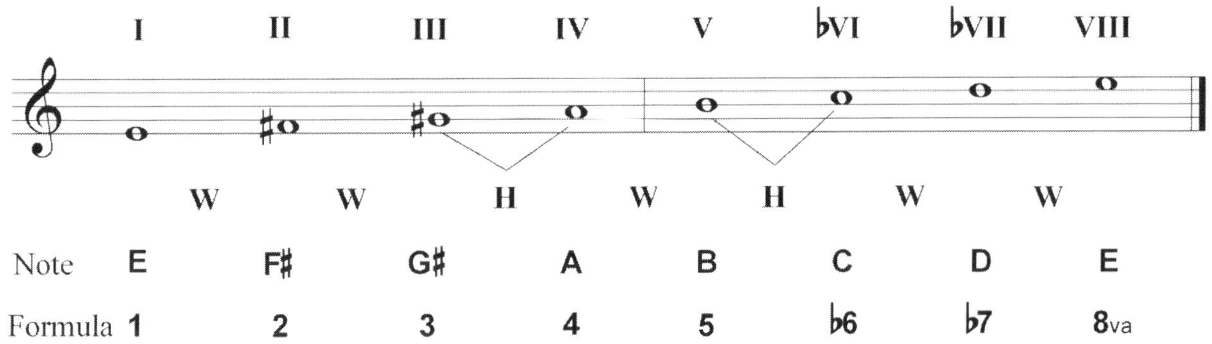

FINGERING OF THE HINDU SCALE

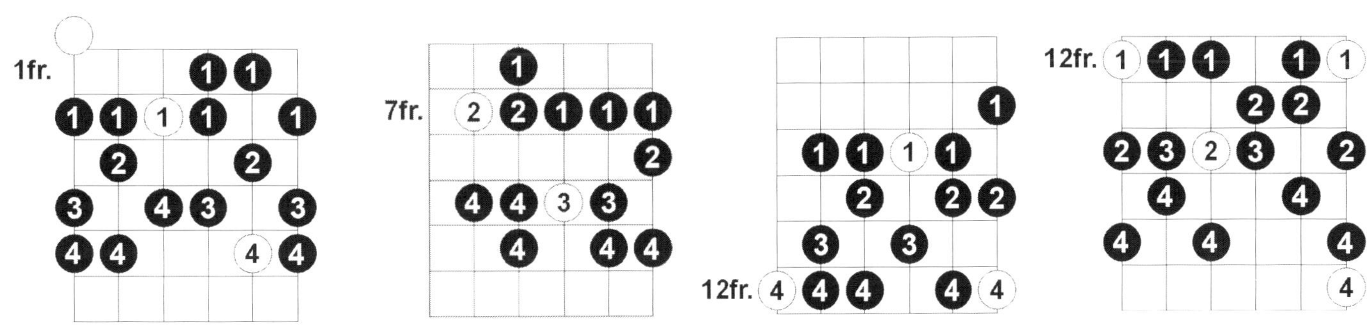

Example 74 **Track 85**

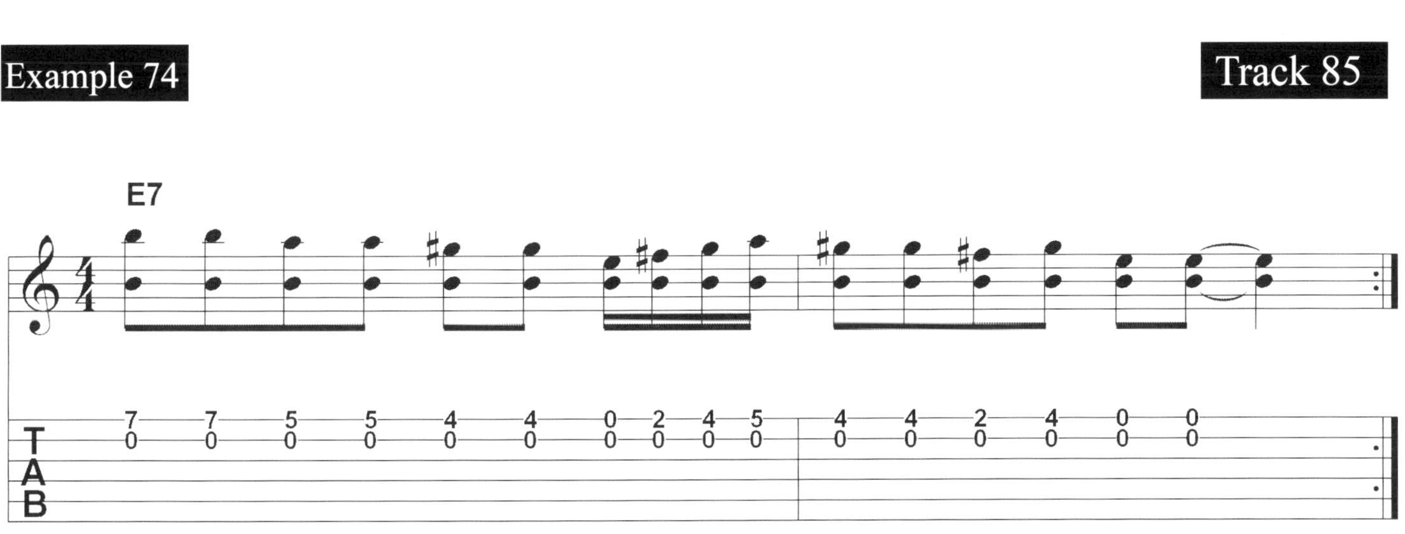

THE SUPER LOCRIAN SCALE

The Super Locrian scale or mode is formed from the seventh degree of the melodic minor scale. From a more practical point of view, to play the Super Locrian scale you only need to play the melodic minor scale a half step higher.
The Super Locrian scale can be applied to dominant 7th and altered dominant chords.

This scale is also known by the following names:

- The **altered scale,** since it contains all possible accidentals **(♭5, 5+, ♭9, 9+).**
- The **diminished-augmented** scale, due to the combination of the diminished scale and the whole-tone scale.
- The **Ravel scale**—so named precisely because it was used by the eminent musician, Maurice Ravel.
- The **Locrian ♭4 scale**, as it contains the notes of the Locrian mode with an added flat-fourth**.**
- The **Pomeroy** scale, after American jazz trumpeter, Herb Pomeroy.

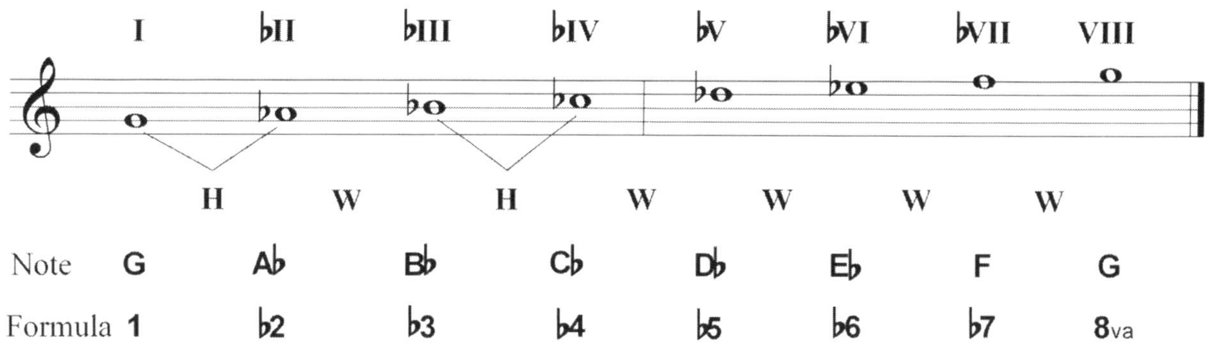

FINGERING OF THE SUPER LOCRIAN SCALE

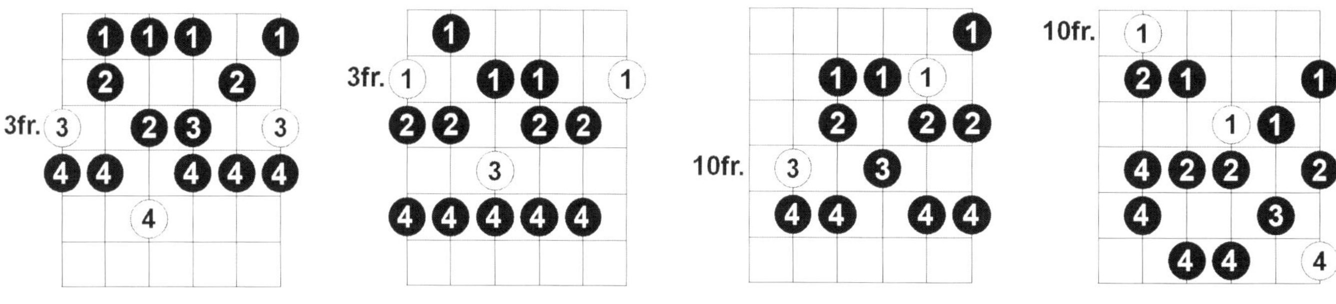

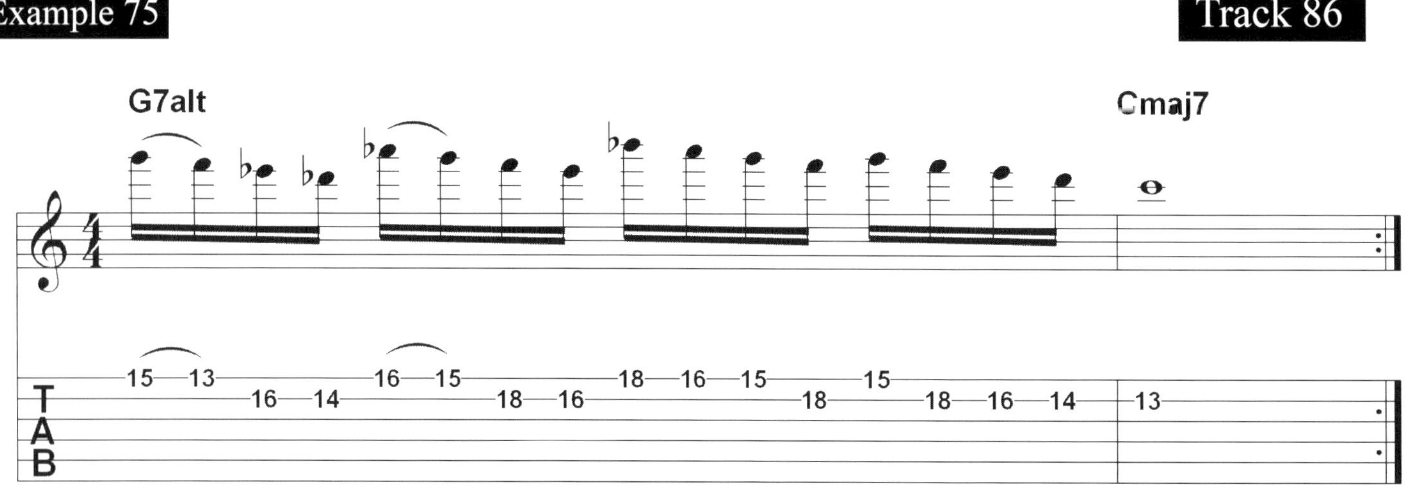

Try playing this next example *staccato* as on the recording.

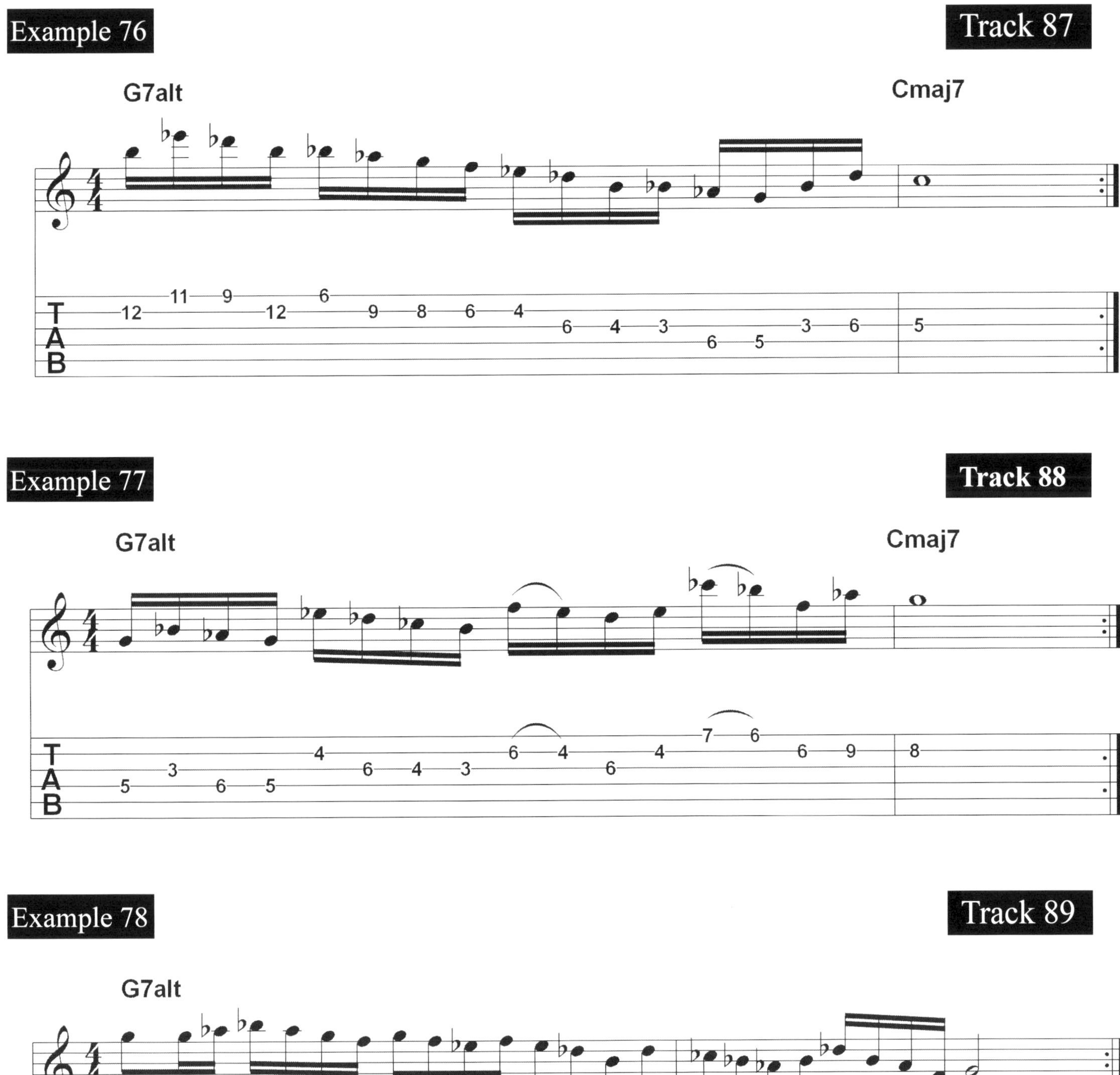

Example 78

Track 89

G7alt

T
A
B

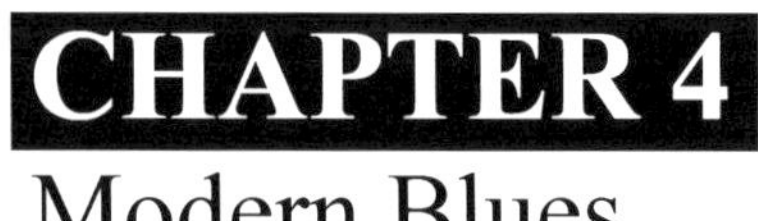

Modern Blues

THE BLUES PROGRESSION

The harmony of a typical blues tune is based on the three primary chords that are built on the I, IV and V degrees of the scale. These chords are usually distributed over a repetitive progression of twelve measures creating a **12-bar blues**, but 8, 16 and 32-measure forms also exist. At the same time, the minor seventh is usually added to these chords, making them all dominant seventh chords. For example, if we are playing in the key of G major, instead of playing G, C and D (I, IV, V) we would play G7, C7 and D7 (I7, IV7, V7); that is why—as an exception to the rule—**in the case of blues, the dominant seventh chord works as a tonic**. The overall effect of unceasing dominant seventh chords is that the harmony never really settles or resolves, and the implied forward motion is constant.

TYPICAL 12-BAR BLUES PROGRESSION IN G

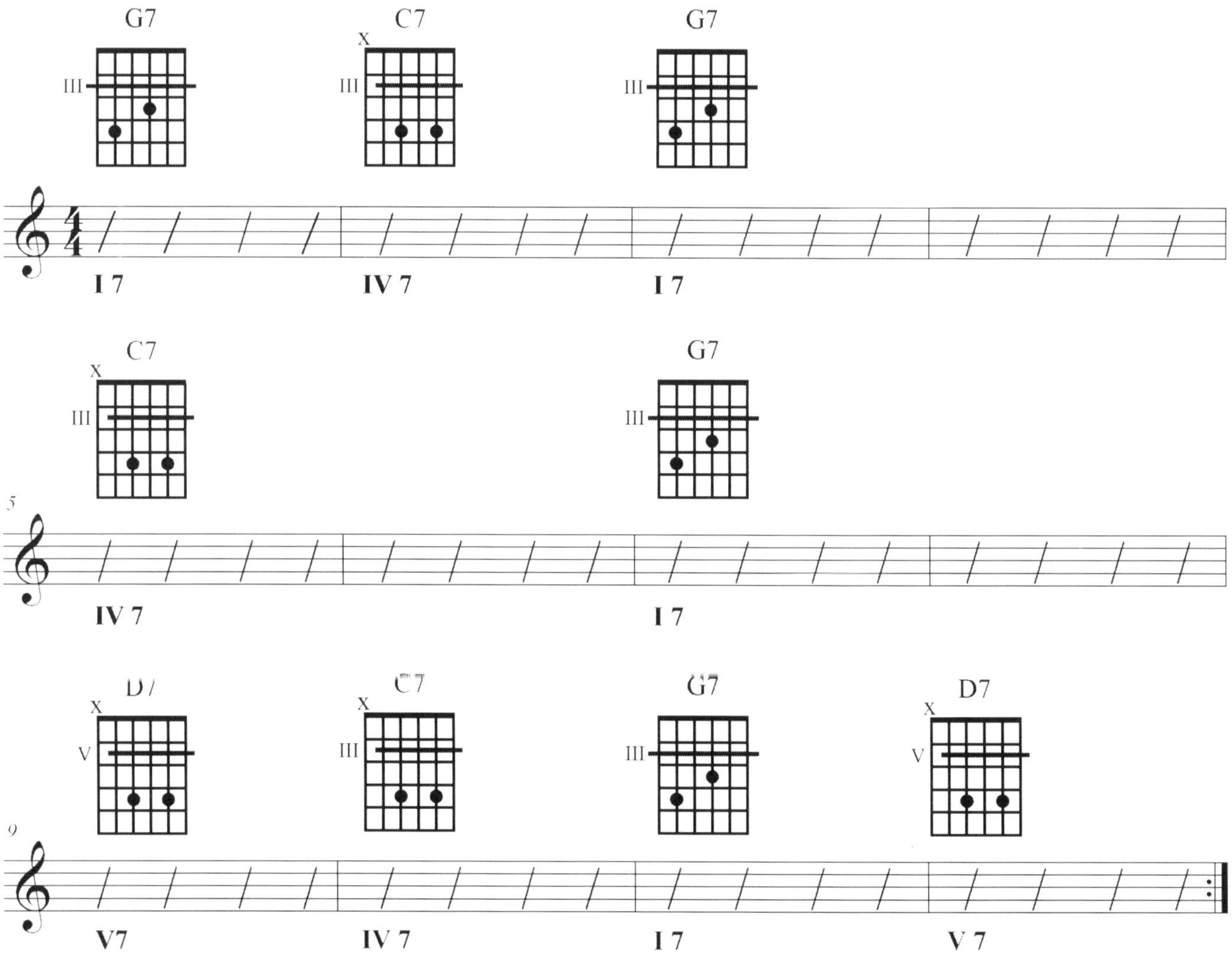

G7 C7 G7

I 7 IV 7 I 7

C7 G7

IV 7 I 7

D7 C7 G7 D7

V7 IV 7 I 7 V 7

FIRST VARIATION

In this first variation of our blues chord progression, we will incorporate additional notes called **extensions (13, 9, ♭9 and ♯9)** over some dominant seventh chords as well as using the diminished chord a half-step above the dominant seventh chord with G♯° replacing G7 in the fourth measure and C♯° replacing C7 in the sixth measure. In measures 11 and 12 we find a **turnaround** which consists of a sequence of chords at the end of the last phrase of the melody that prepares the listener for the repeat of the theme but avoids certain monotony.

TYPICAL 12-BAR BLUES PROGRESSION IN G
VARIATION 1

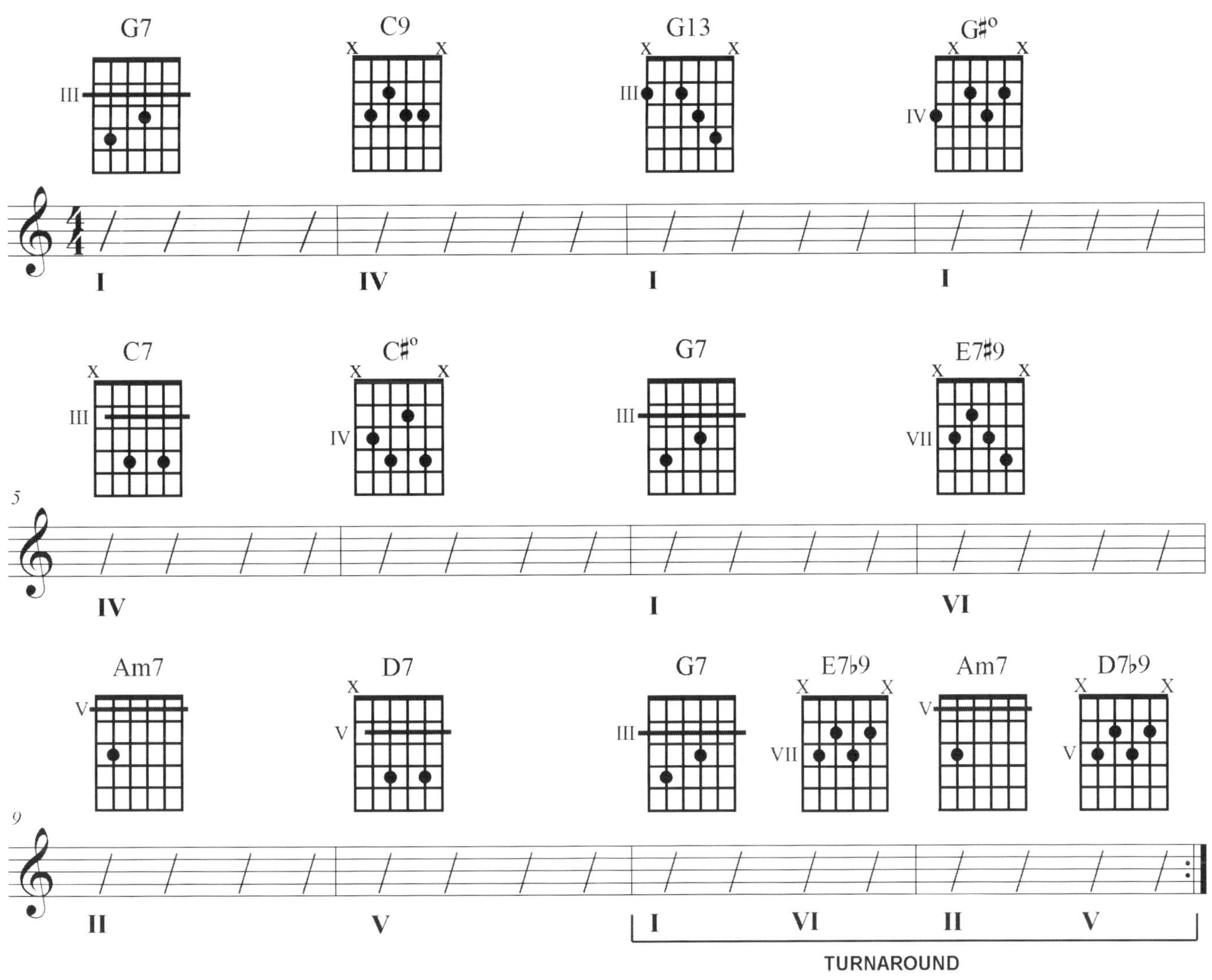

SECOND VARIATION

In this second variation, we will make use of the respective **tritone substitutions** for the main chords as well as for the secondary ones. In the following example D♭7 is substituted for G7 in the second half of measure 1. This seems an odd match to make as the two chords have no common tones. The reason this change "works" is that both the G7 and D♭7 chords have common tones with the C chord that follows and an engaging chromatic bass line (D-D♭-C) is also possible. This type of harmony is very common in jazz; here, we will use this device in a blues context, but in more of a jazz style.

For more information on substitutions, see Mel Bay's *Jazz Theory Handbook* (97845M) by Peter Spitzer.

TYPICAL 12-BAR BLUES PROGRESSION IN G
VARIATION 2 WITH TRITONE SUBSTITUTIONS

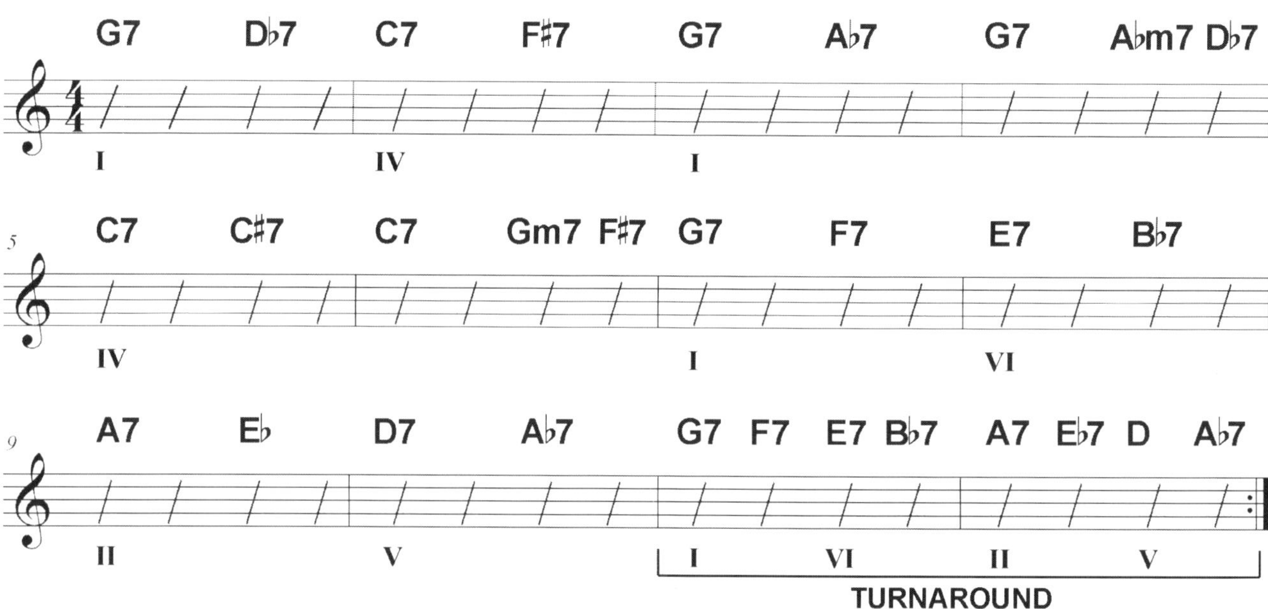

The following patterns are built on the **G Major** pentatonic scale

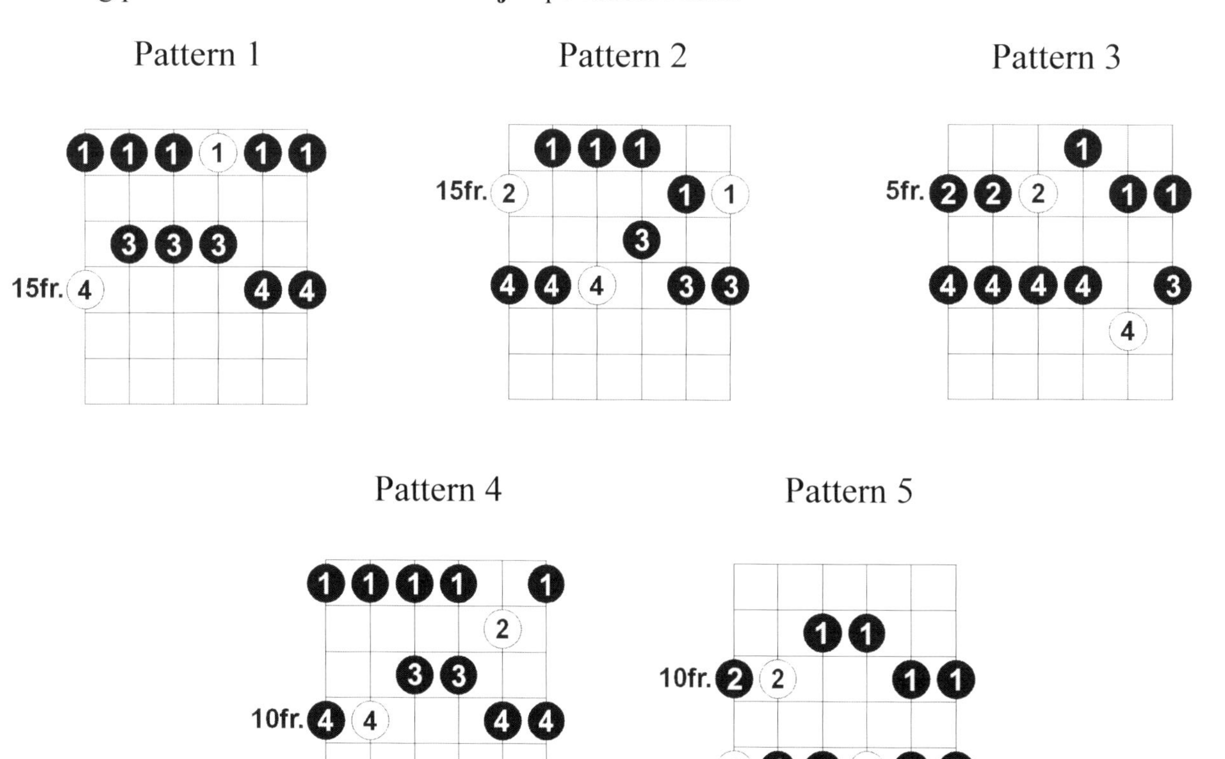

The following patterns are built on the **E Minor** pentatonic scale

Pattern 1

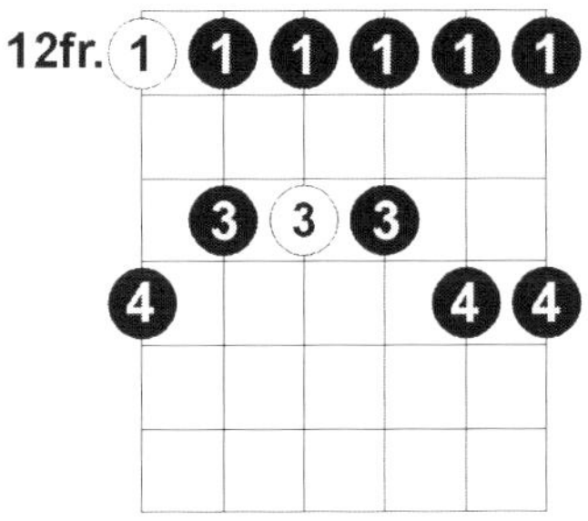

12fr.

Pattern 2

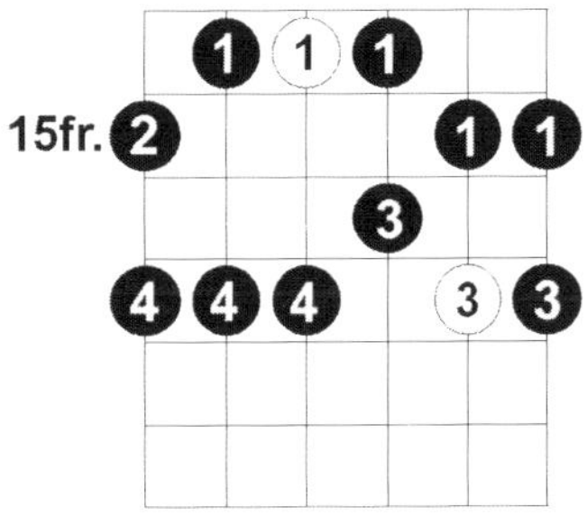

15fr.

Pattern 3

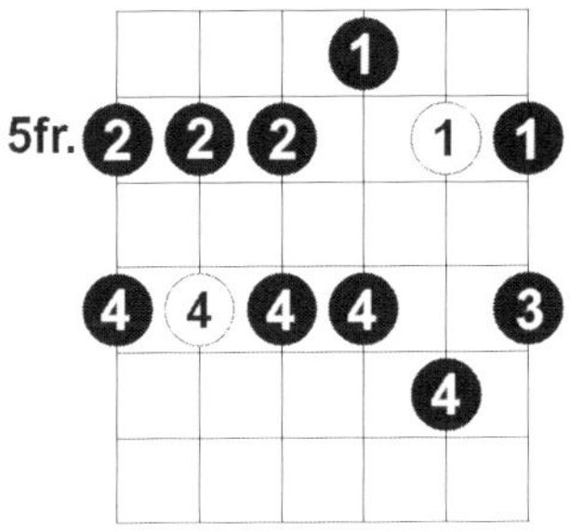

5fr.

Pattern 4

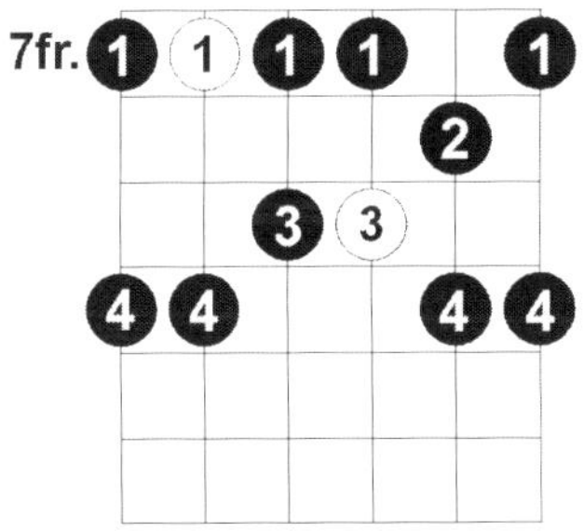

7fr.

Pattern 5

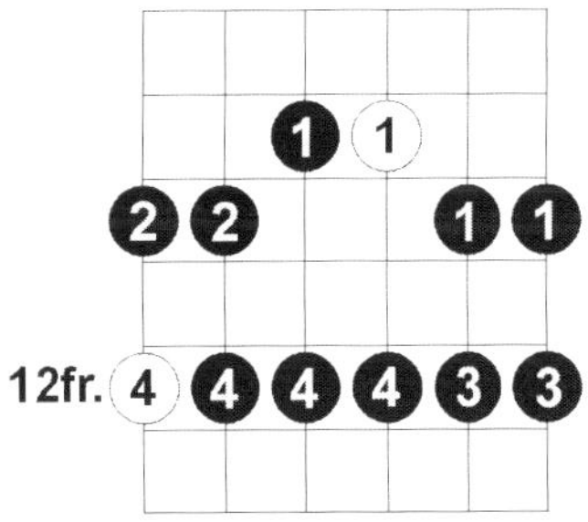

12fr.

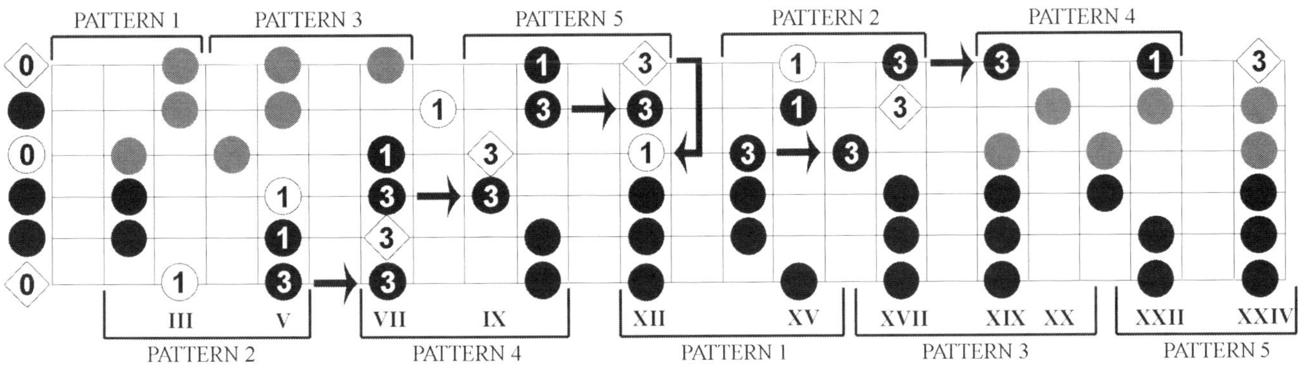

PATTERN 1 PATTERN 3 PATTERN 5 PATTERN 2 PATTERN 4

III V VII IX XII XV XVII XIX XX XXII XXIV

PATTERN 2 PATTERN 4 PATTERN 1 PATTERN 3 PATTERN 5

◇ The diamonds indicate the E minor tonics.

○ The white circles indicate the G major tonics.

Next, we will see some melodic ideas that can be applied to the first four measures of our blues, using different types of scales, modes and arpeggios.

Example 79

Track 90

In the first example we use the G minor pentatonic scale (**G-B♭-C-D-F**) over the first four measures. Play this one using swing eighths. Notice the quartertone bend in the second measure.

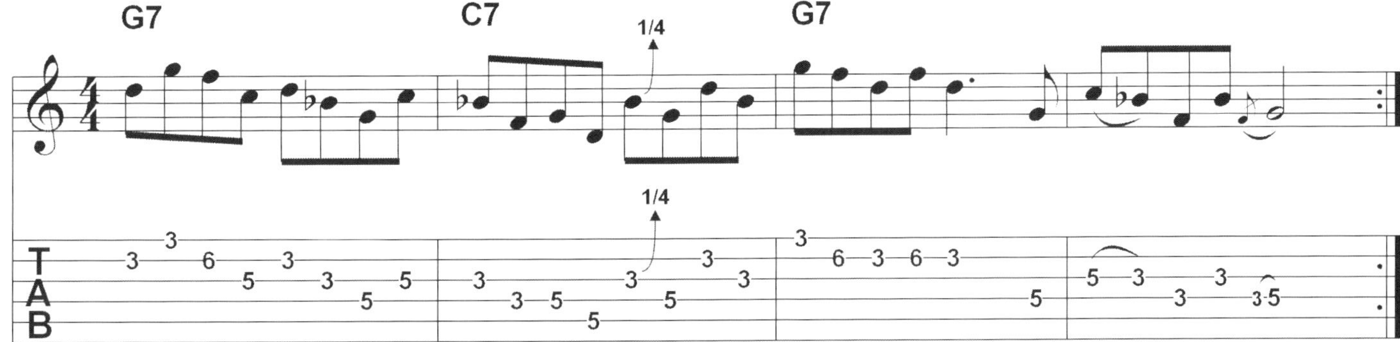

Example 80

Track 91

In the following example we again use the G minor pentatonic scale during the first measures of our blues. **When improvising, pay attention to the chord changes and build similar phrases.**

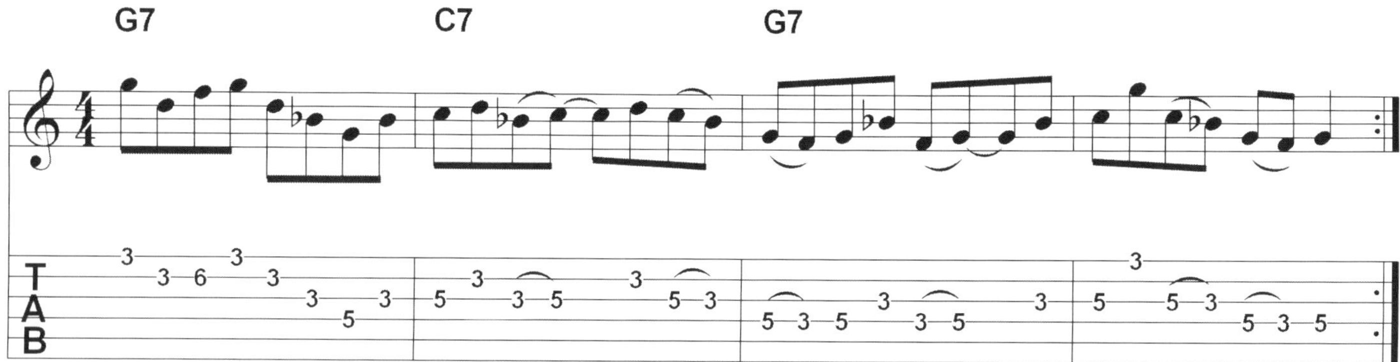

Example 81

Track 92

In the next phrase we play the G minor pentatonic scale **(G-B♭-C-D-F)** over the G7 chord and the C minor pentatonic scale **(C-E♭-F-G-B♭)** over the C7 chord.

Example 82

Track 93

Here, we use the G major pentatonic scale **(G-A-B-D-E)** over the first four measures of our blues. **Build similar ideas for the entire progression.**

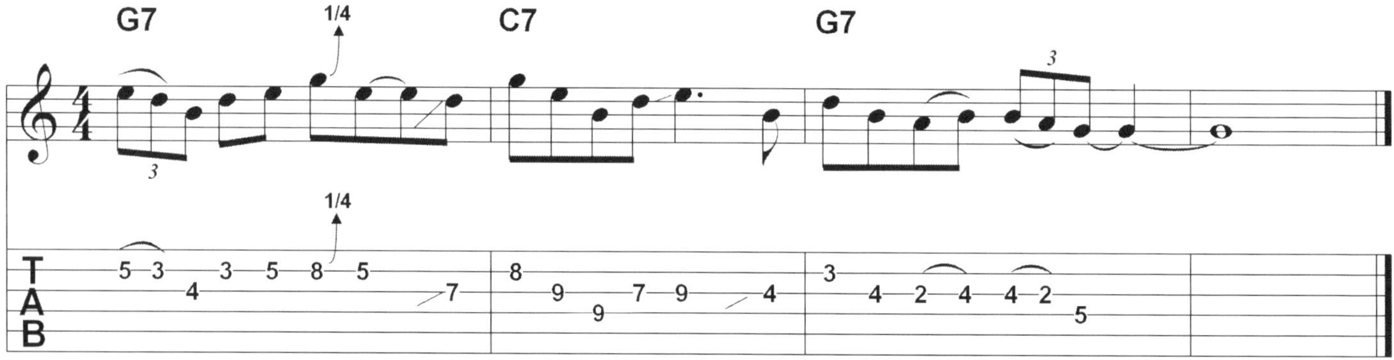

Example 83

Track 94

Next, we play the G major pentatonic scale **(G-A-B-D-E)** over the G7 chord and the C major pentatonic scale **(C-D-E-G-A)** over the C7 chord.

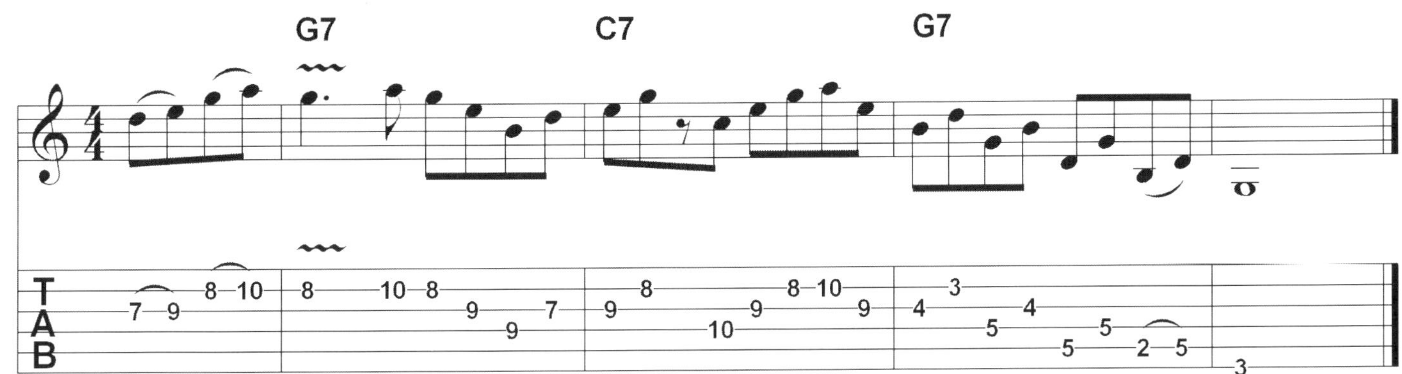

Example 84

Track 95

Now we play the blues minor scale over the first 4 measures. This is a minor pentatonic scale with the addition of its augmented fourth or diminished fifth, thus generating a 6-tone scale: **(G-B♭-C-C♯-D-F).**
This scale is applied to dominant seventh and minor 7th chords.

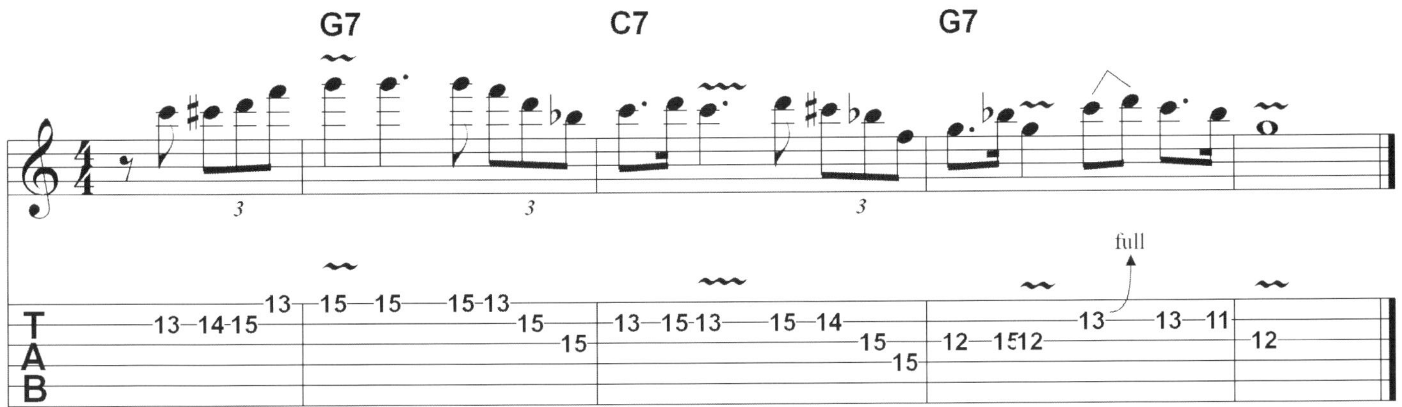

Example 85

Track 96

Here, we again use the blues minor scale over the first 4 measures.
It is important to remember that both the minor third, the diminished fifth and the minor seventh are considered "blue notes".

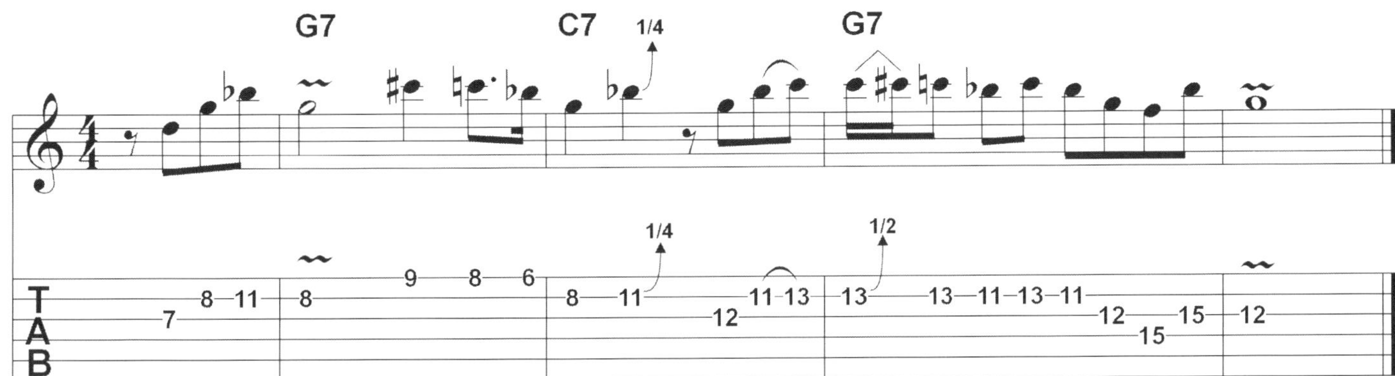

Example 86

Track 97

In the following example we play the G minor blues scale **(G-B♭-C-C♯-D-F)** over the G7 chord and the C minor blues scale **(C-E♭-F-F♯-G-B♭)** over the C7 chord.

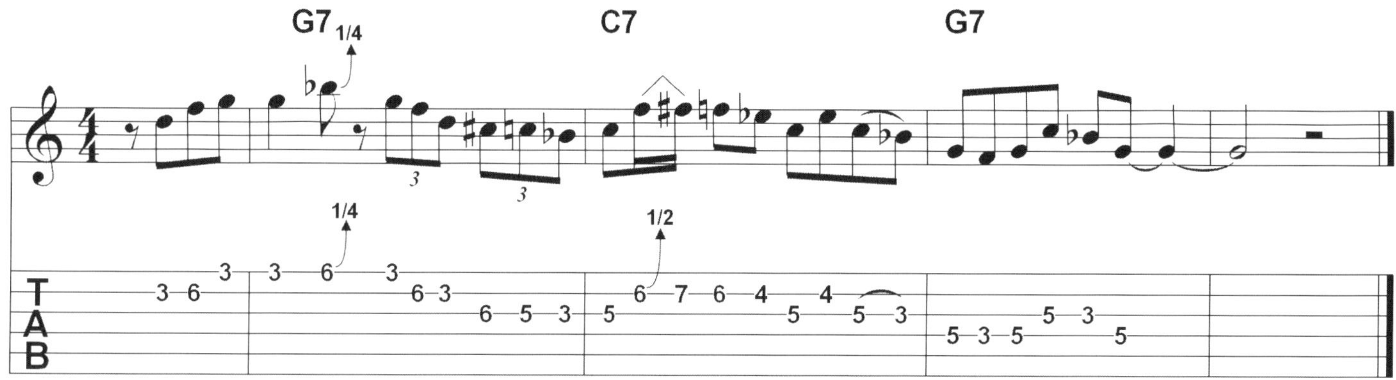

Example 87

Track 98

In the following example, we again apply the blues major scale. This is a major pentatonic scale with the addition of its augmented second degree (2+) or its minor third (flat-3), generating a chromatic passage between degrees II and III. Play the G major blues scale **(G-A-B♭-B-D-E)** over the G7 chord and the C major blues scale **(C-D-E♭-E-G-A)** over the C7 chord.

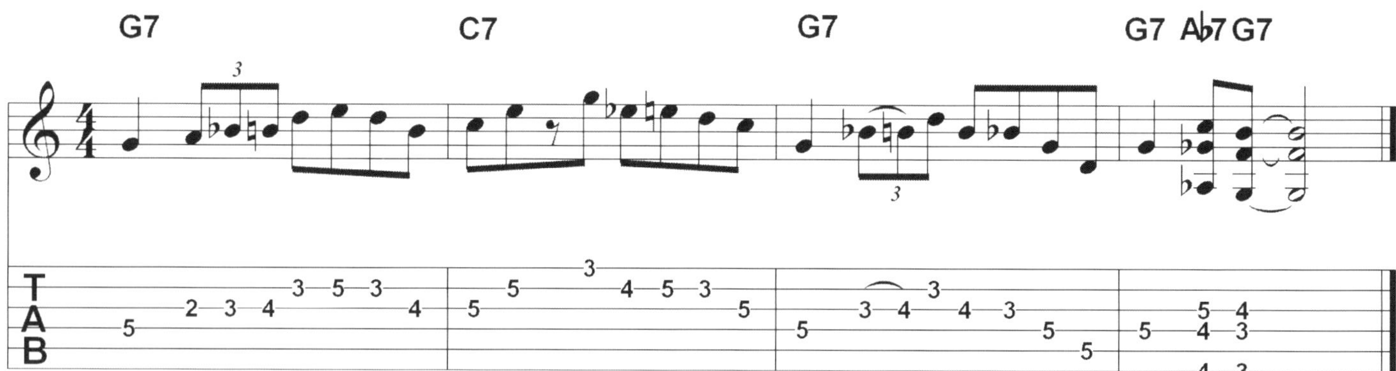

Example 88

Track 99

In the following phrase we use a very interesting resource; we play the G minor pentatonic scale with the addition of its major third, resulting in the following notes: G-B♭-B-C-D-F.

Play and improvise with this scale in all positions.

Example 89

Track 100

Here is a new phrase applying the scale from the previous example.
Control the pitch when bending!

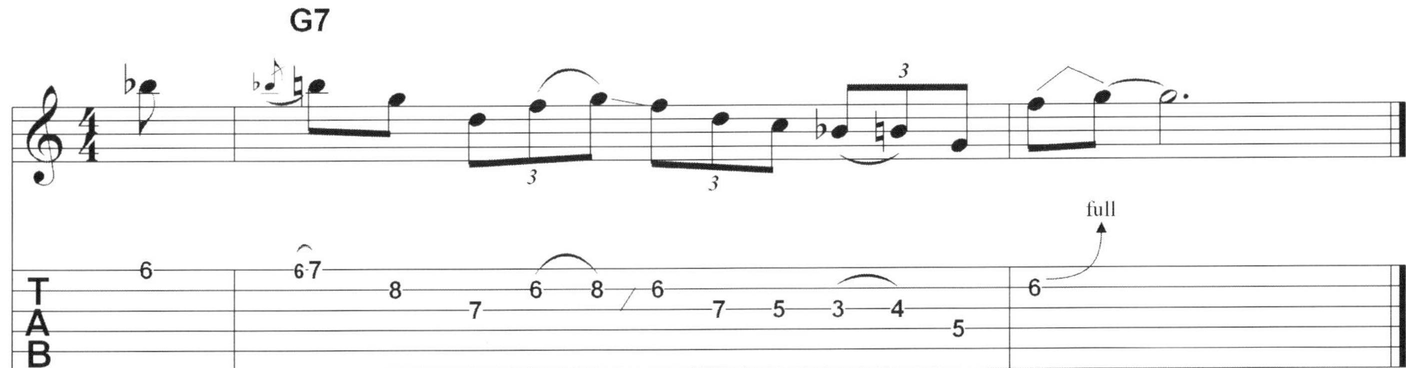

Example 90

Track 101

Here's another new phrase using the G minor pentatonic scale plus the addition of its major third.
Play with this scale and compose your own phrases!

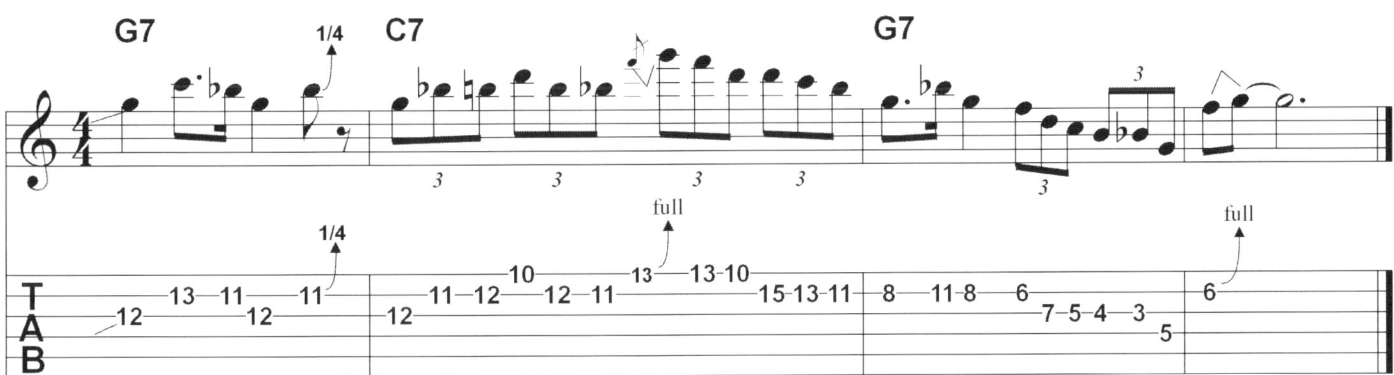

Example 91

Track 102

Another interesting approach when improvising in blues is to play the minor pentatonic scale but replacing its minor seventh with the major sixth, resulting in a scale with the following notes: G-B♭-C-D-E.

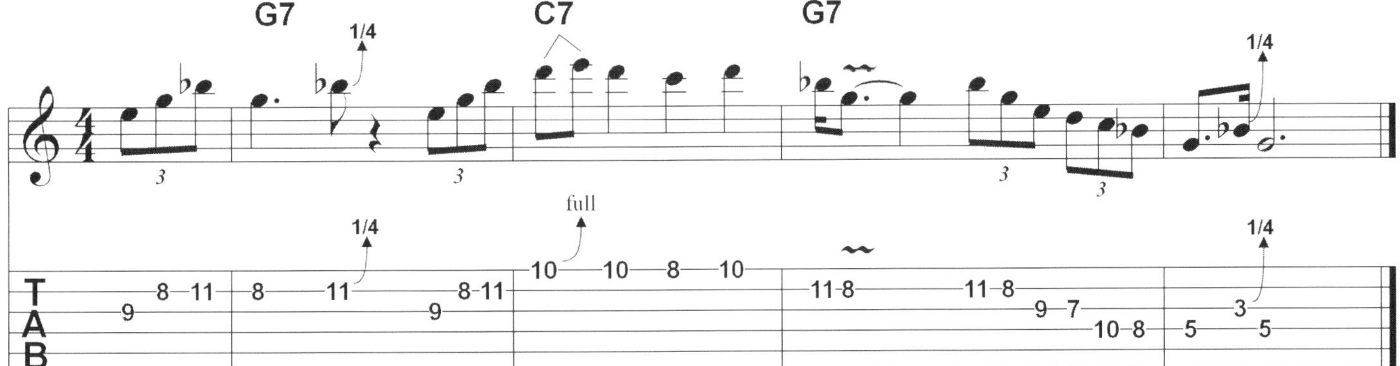

Example 92

Track 103

Here's a new phrase applying the same concept as the previous exercise.
Again, play with this scale and compose your own phrases!

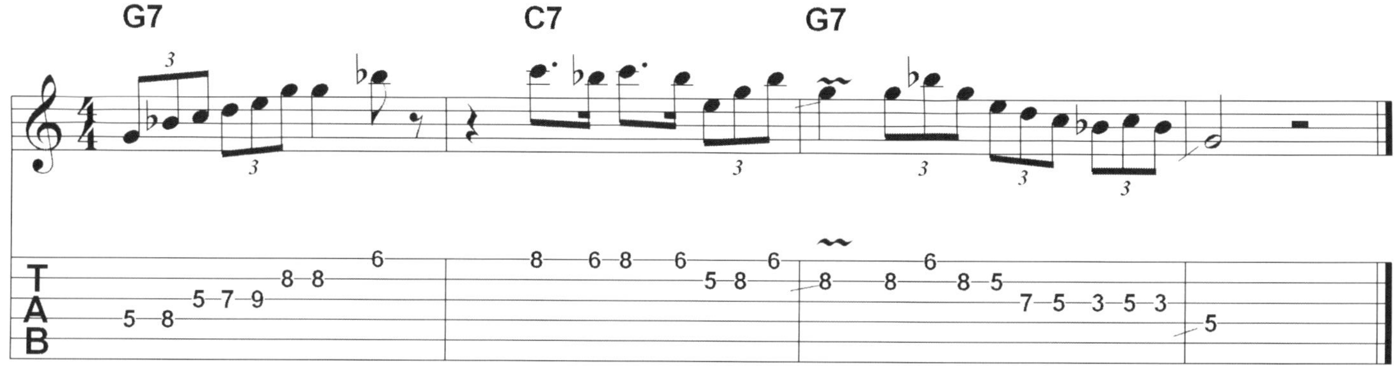

In the following example we incorporate the **whole-tone scale** of G **(G-A-B-C♯-D♯-F-G)** in our blues. This scale is constructed of six whole tones; the whole-tone scale, together with the diminished scale and the chromatic scale, form a group of scales known as **symmetrical scales**. The unique thing about this scale is that no matter where we start, we hear the same interval from note to note. Generally, this scale is applied to altered dominant chords.

Although the whole-tone scale was used by several composers in the 20th century, perhaps the main one we associate with it is Claude Debussy who made effective use of this scale in many of his compositions.

Example 93

Track 104

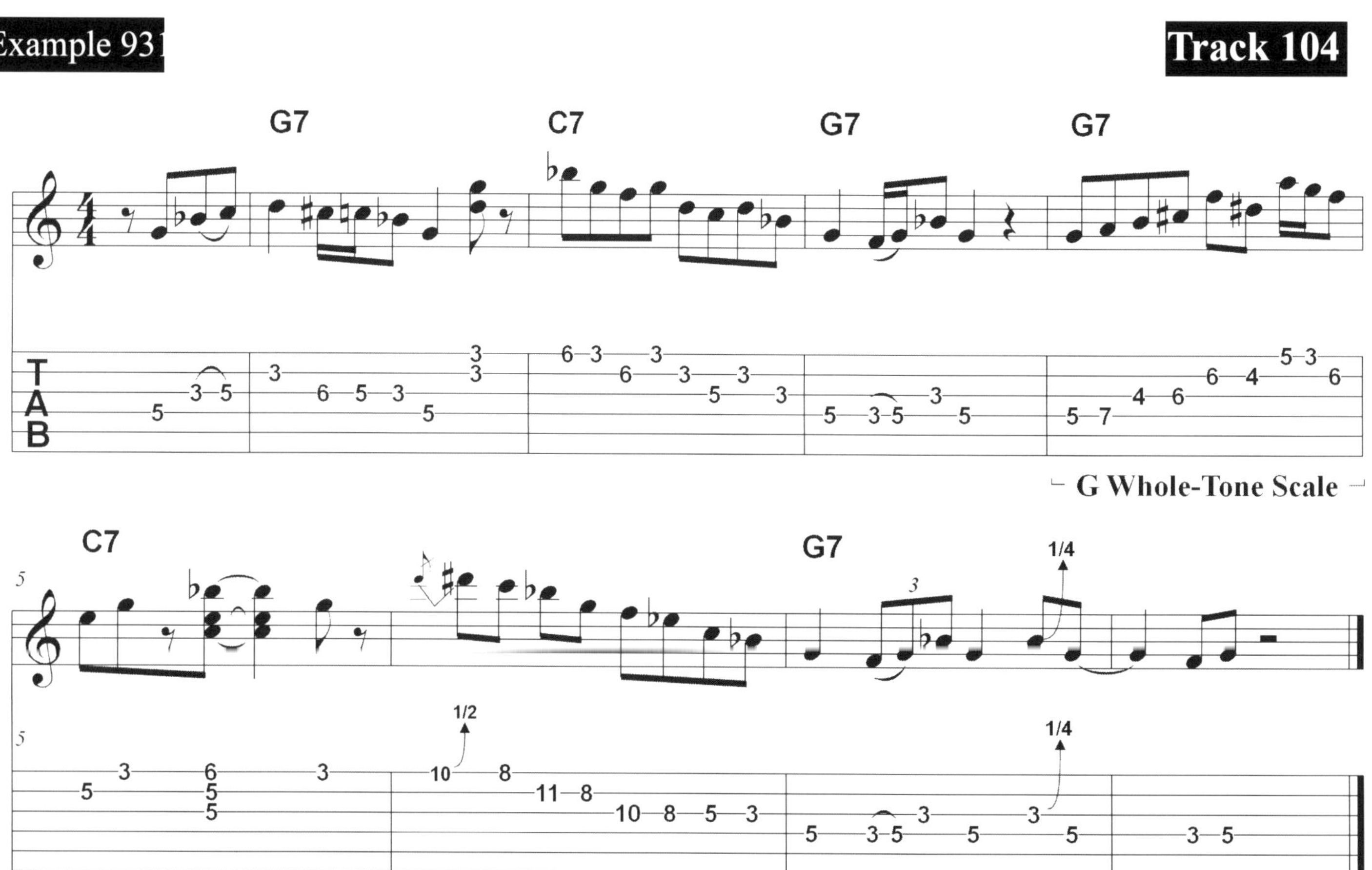

In the next example we incorporate the **diminished scale** in our blues. This scale is composed of whole steps and half steps used alternately as follows: whole-step, half-step, whole-step, half-step, etc. Depending on how it is applied, it can also start with a half-step: half-step, whole-step, half-step, whole-step, etc. This scale corresponds to the so-called **symmetrical scales** and is characterized by containing eight notes:
(G♯-A♯-B-C♯-D-E-F-G).
The diminished scale is usually used on diminished chords, as well as on dominant seventh chords.
In the examples we apply the diminished G♯ scale (half-step, whole step) in the fourth measure and the C♯ diminished scale (half step, whole step) in the sixth measure.

Example 94 **Track 105**

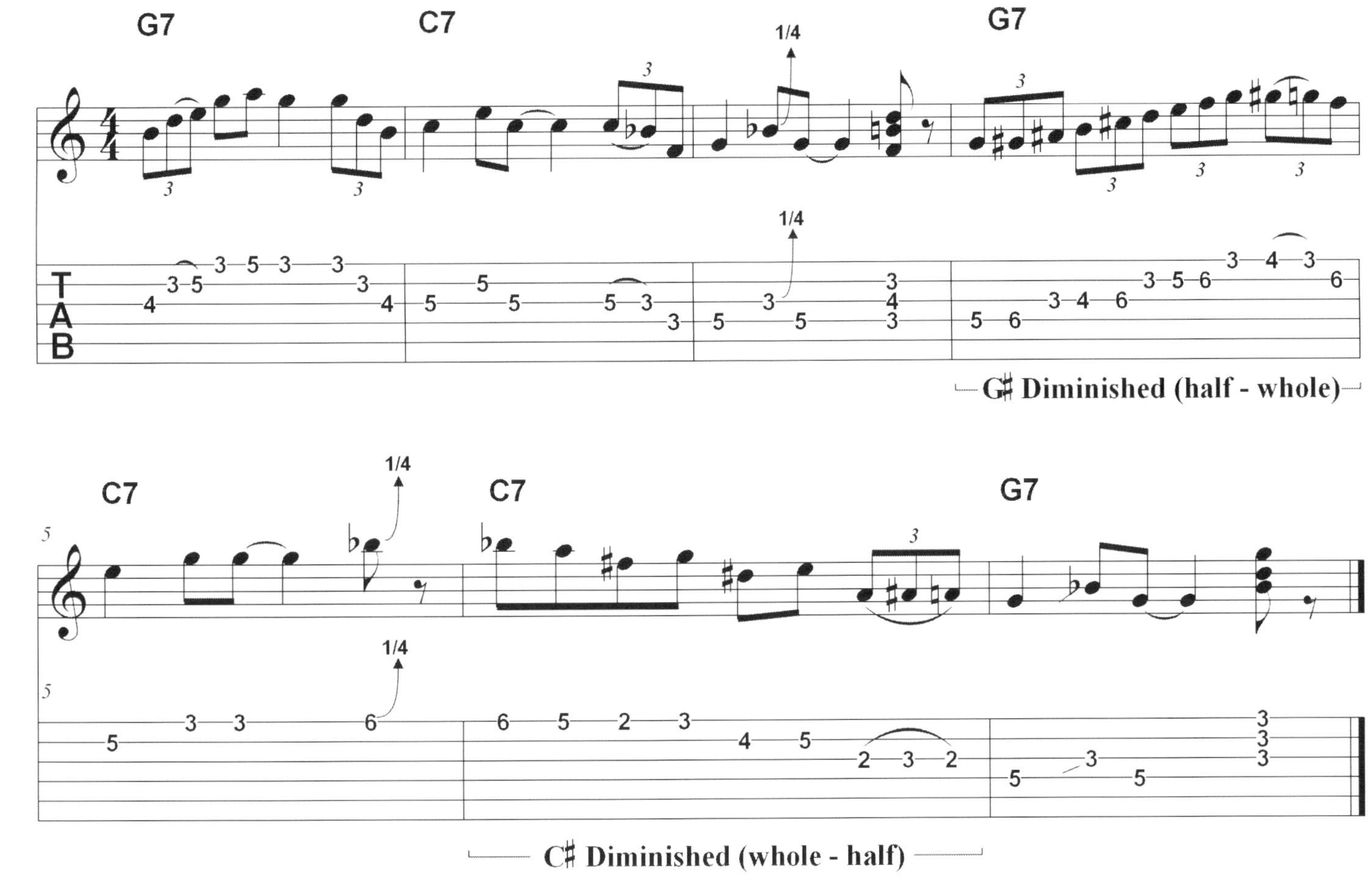

G7 C7 G7

G♯ Diminished (half - whole)

C7 C7 G7

C♯ Diminished (whole - half)

Example 95 **Track 106**

In the following phrase, we use G Mixolydian mode **(G-A-B-C-D-E-F-G)** in the first measure.

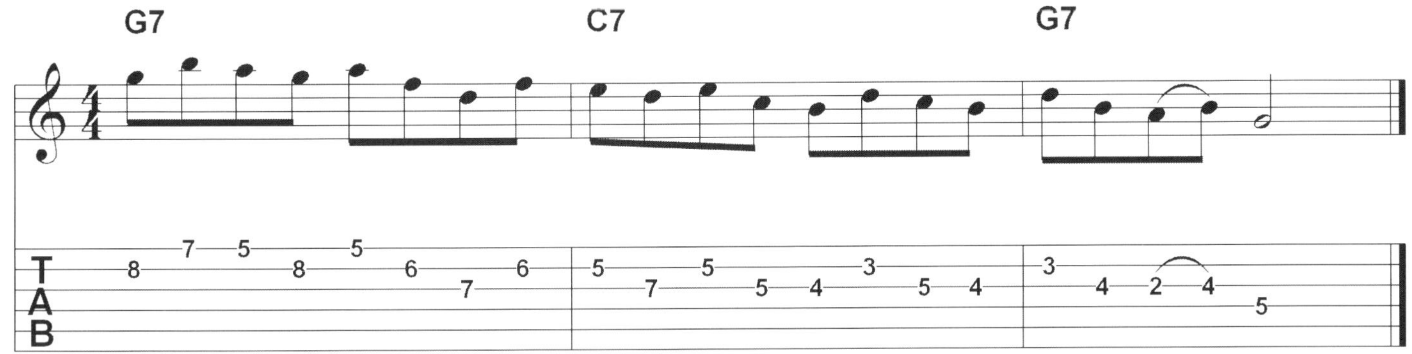

Example 96 **Track 107**

Here, we use the mixolydian mode of G **(G-A-B-C-D-E-F-G)** over G7 and play the mixolydian mode of C **(C-D-E-F-G-A-B♭-C)** over the C7 chord. **Compose similar phrases of your own!**

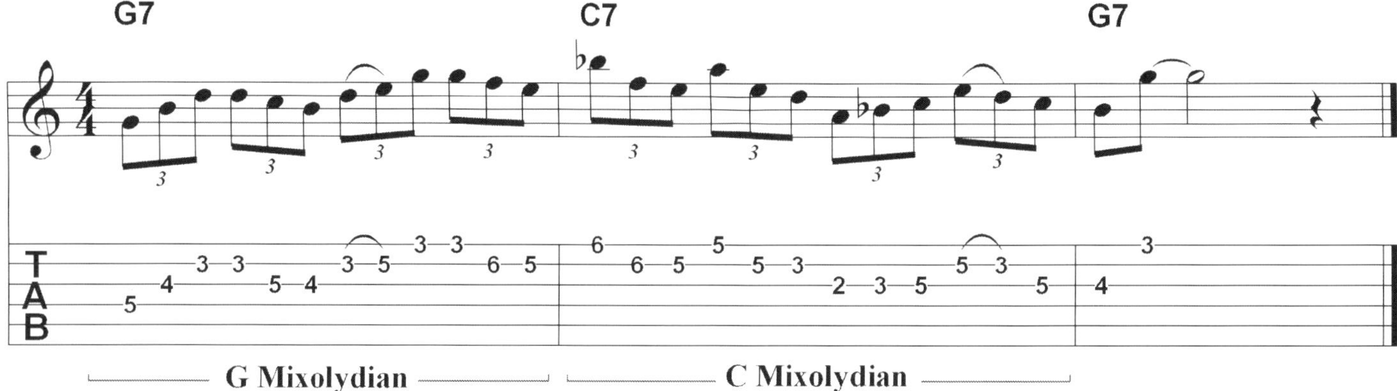

Example 97 **Track 108**

In the following progression we use the Lydian flat-7 scale. This scale, also known as the **overtone scale**, is the fourth mode of the melodic minor scale and its formula is **(1-2-3-4♯-5-6-♭7)**. We can see that it differs from the Mixolydian mode because it contains an augmented fourth degree that is easy to remember when fingering it. The main use of this scale is with substituted dominants, as the following example shows us, since the tension ♯11 (sharp - 11, G) is the fundamental of the substituted dominant (G7).

Example 98 **Track 109**

In blues, the Lydian ♭7 scale is usually applied on the IV7 chord (blues subdominant).
In Examples 98, 99 and 100 we play the C Lydian ♭7 scale **(C-D-E-F♯-G-A-B♭-C),** the fourth mode of the G melodic minor scale **(G-A-B♭-C-D-E-F♯-G)** over the C7 chord.

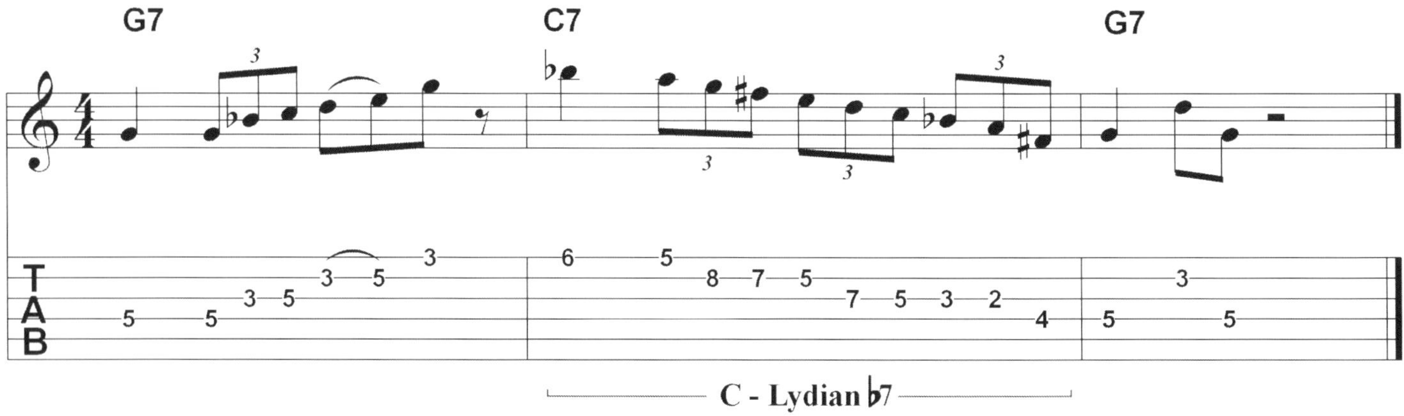

Track 110

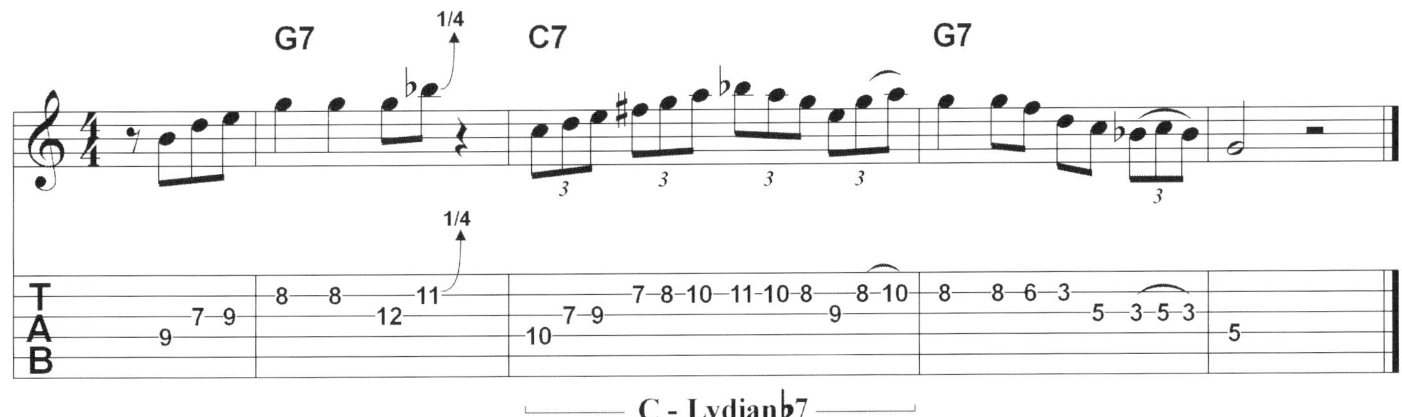

Example 100

Track 111

Example 101

Track 112

In the following example we use the G Super Locrian modal scale over the fourth measure of our blues. Scales that alter the Mixolydian mode are usually used over measures 1, 4 and 12.

In these last examples we incorporate arpeggios in our blues progression.

Example 102

Track 113

Here, we play the G7 arpeggio **(G-B-D-F)** over the G7 chord and the Cmi9 arpeggio **(C-E♭-G-B♭-D)** over the C7 chord.

Example 103

Track 114

In the next phrase, we start by playing the G major pentatonic scale over the first measure. Then we play the C7 arpeggio **(C-E-G-B♭)** over the C7 chord and the G7 arpeggio **(G-B-D-F)** over the G7.

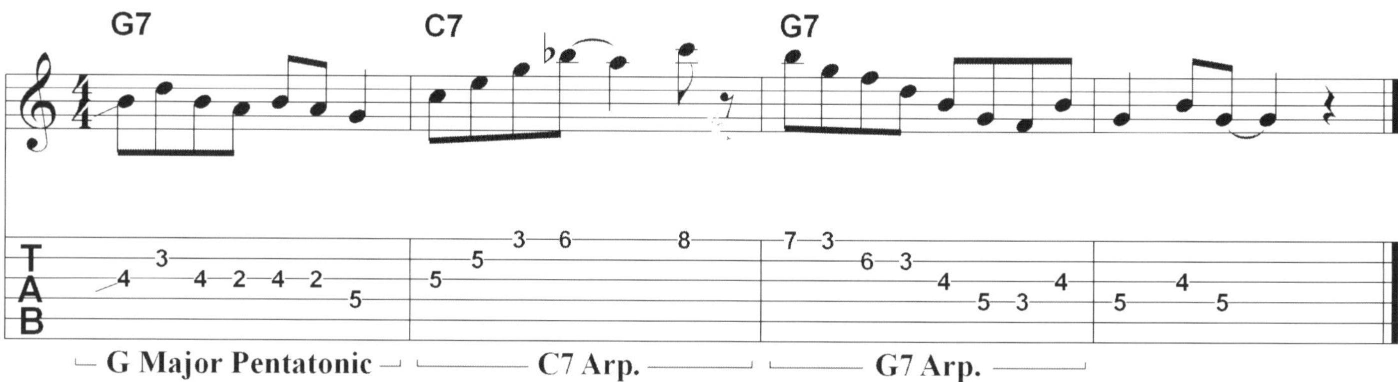

Example 104

Track 115

Continue using the G7 and C7 arpeggios over the respective chords.

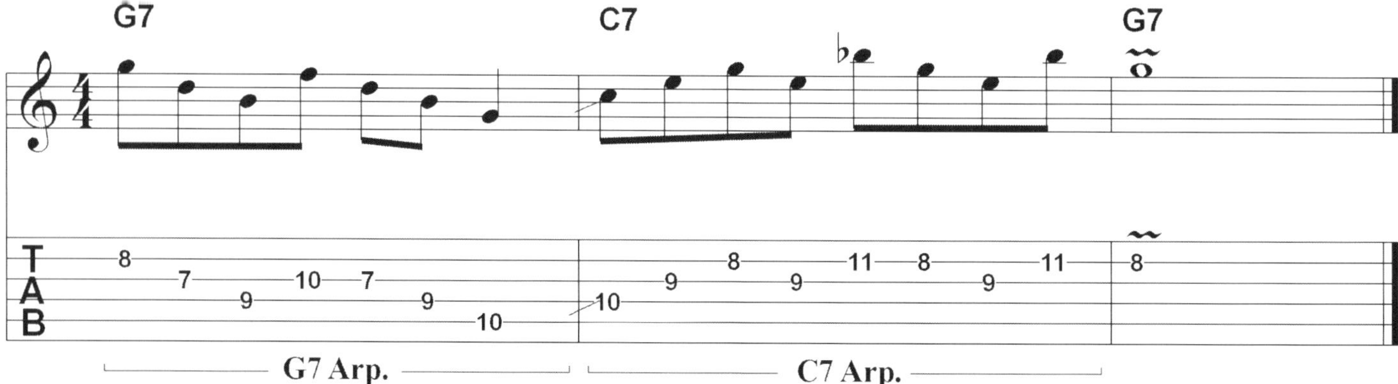

Example 105

Track 116

Here is a new phrase using the arpeggios corresponding to each chord.
In keeping with these examples, compose your own blues phrases.

Example 106

Track 117

In the following example, we play the Dmi9 arpeggio over the G7 chord and the Gmi9 arpeggio over the C7 chord.
Incorporate these ideas in your own improvisations.

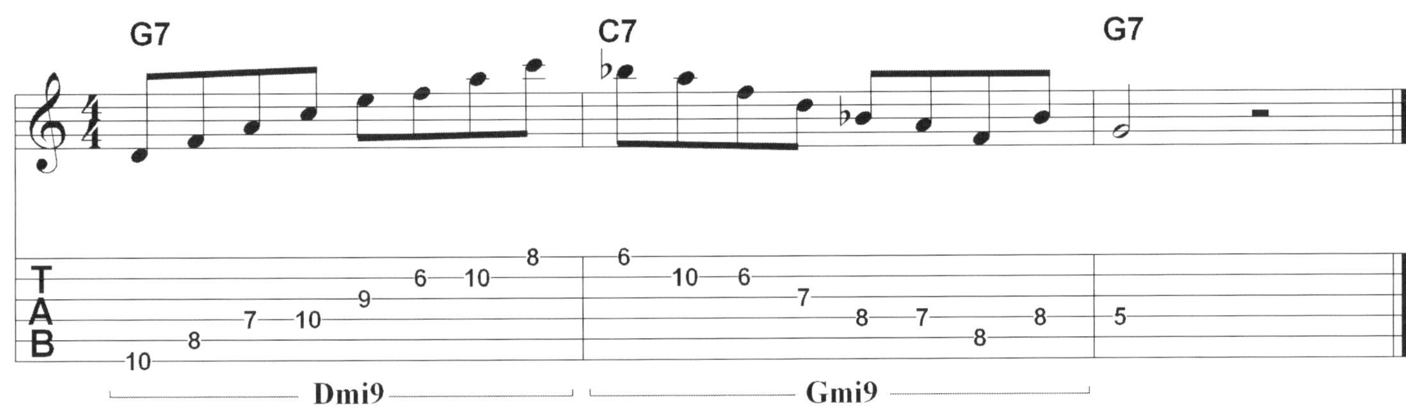

Example 107

Track 118

The following example illustrates the use of arpeggios in a blues-jazz fusion progression.

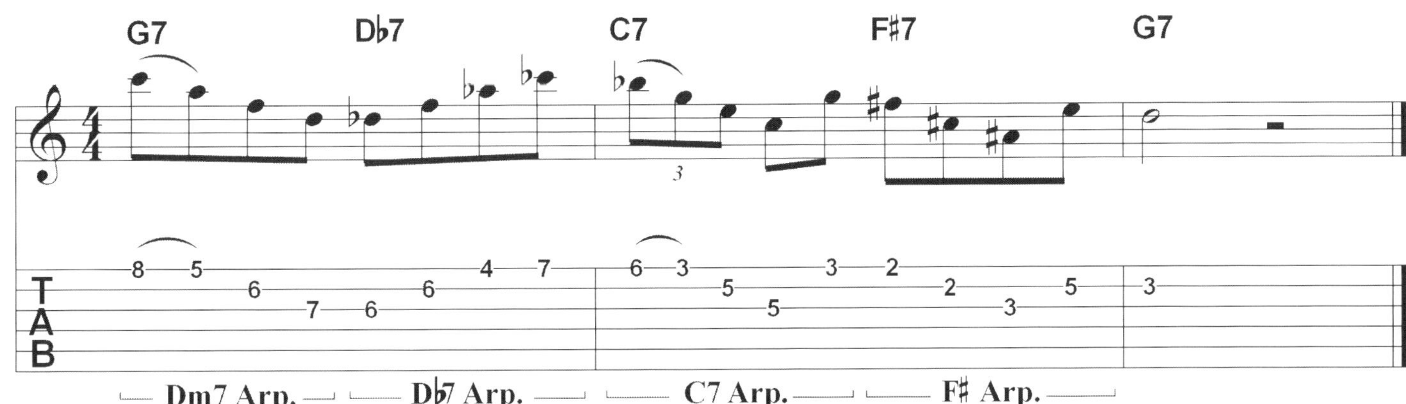

Example 108

Track 119

In the first measure, we play the G and A♭m7 arpeggios over the G7 chord; then we play the C7 and F♯7 arpeggios over the C7 chord.

Example 109

Track 120

We end with a **Blues in G**, applying some of the melodic ideas introduced in this chapter.

Study all the scales, modes and arpeggios introduced in this book; then, compose your own phrases to strengthen your rock solos and blues improvisations. With these tools in your pocket, you'll never be stuck at Robert Johnson's "Blues Crossroads"—unless you are attending the outstanding blues festival in Clarksdale, Mississippi.

BLUES IN G

About the Author

Born in Buenos Aires Argentina in 1974, Pablo Pescatore first became interested in the guitar at age 14 while listening to bands like Iron Maiden, Kiss, AC/DC, and the German hard-rock band, The Scorpions; it was when he heard Deep Purple with Richie Blackmore, however, that he decided to dedicate himself fully to music. Then, when he heard Yngwie Malmsteen, everything changed, and he spent many hours studying Malmsteen's unusual techniques.

Pablo then enrolled in the EFIMUS school for the formation of professional musicians where over the next ten years he studied guitar, music theory and harmony and attended courses and masterclasses on various instruments and musical styles, including blues, jazz and bossa-nova. He graduated with honors in 2000 with a degree as a "Professor of Guitar, Harmony and Solfege". After graduation, Pablo worked as a studio musician and played with various bands and as a soloist in different styles; he has written several books on guitar technique for Crisal De Roca Publishing as well as writing a column for the prestigious Mexican magazine, *GuitarraMx*. Pablo's first book with Mel Bay Publications, *The Complete Book of Shred Guitar (30693M)* was released in 2019.

For the past 30-plus years he has taught classical and rock guitar courses and masterclasses in different music academies and conservatories in Ecuador, Honduras, Mexico, and the United States, not to mention giving private lessons in his hometown of Buenos Aires.

Pablo adds:

> Although I have been involved with rock music for most of my professional career, I also love classical music, mainly the music of Bach, Vivaldi, Beethoven, Mozart, and Paganini. Aside from music, I am passionate about soccer. If I had not become a musician, I think I would have dedicated myself to this sport. I still love to play soccer with friends. I am also very interested in automotive design, and purely as therapy, I really enjoy cooking. Apart from spending the balance of my time with my wife and three children, I am an artist-signature endorser of Skull Strings electric guitar strings, actively engaged in recording new solo projects.
>
> Thank you for your interest in my publishing and recording concepts!
>
> All best wishes and *un abrazo*,
> Pablo Pescatore

Other Mel Bay Rock Guitar Books

The Complete Book of Shred Guitar/El Libro Completo de Guitarra Shred (Pescatore)
3rd Millennium Guitar: An Introduction to Perfect 4th Tuning (Law)
Advanced Modern Rock Guitar Improvisation (Finn)
Altered States (Delach)
Blues Jam Play-Along Vol. 1 (W. Bay)
Blues Jam Play-Along Vol. 2 (W. Bay)
Electric Blues Guitar Workout (Bowden)
Expanding Your Soloing (Reed)
Fundamentals of Guitar (Miles Okazaki)
Guide to Guitar Chord Progressions (M. Christiansen)
Improvising Without Scales (Verheyen)
Introduction to Harmony for Guitar with Tab (McDonald)
Killer Technique: Electric Guitar (V. Tkachenka/C. Christiansen)
Learn to Burn: How to Play Fast Using Speed Bursts for Stringed Instruments (C. Bay)
Mel Bay Guitar University Rock Curriculum: Vol. 1/Fluid Soloing (Quinn)
Mel Bay Guitar University Rock Curriculum: Vol. 2/Fluid Pentatonics (Quinn)
Mel Bay Guitar University Rock Curriculum: Vol. 3/Fluid Soloing (Quinn)
Mel Bay Guitar University Rock Curriculum: Vol. 4/Fluid Soloing (Quinn)
Blues/Rock Guitar Improv (Finn)
Practical Sweep Picking for Guitar (Donovan)
Rock/Fusion Improvising (Filipiak)
Rock Guitar Essentials: Gig Savers Complete Edition (C. Christiansen)
Rock Guitar Workout (Delatch)
Rock Lead Scales for Guitar (M. Christiansen)
The Complete Guide to Roots Style Guitar (Rossano)
The Open Tunings Guitar Encyclopedia (Mohr and Klein)
Achieving Guitar Artistry - Contemporary Picking Etudes (Pennanen)
Advanced Modern Rock Guitar Improvisation (Finn)
Beginning Rock/Pop Guitar Etudes (Douglass)
Blues Guitar Made Easy (C. Christiansen)
Electric Baroque (Kiefer)
Etudes Electric (Kiefer)
Guitar Journals: Blues (Multiple Authors)
Guitar Journals: Rock (Multiple Authors)
J. S. Bach for Electric Guitar (Kiefer)
Modern Guitar Method Grade 1: Learn Rock Favorites (C. Bay)
Modern Guitar Method Grade 1: Play All-Time Favorite Hits by Ear (C. Bay)
Modern Guitar Method Grade 3: Rock Studies (Multiple Authors)
Modern Guitar Method Grade 4: Rock Studies (Multiple Authors)
Rock Guitar Made Easy (C. Christiansen)
Traditional Music of the British Isles for Electric Guitar/Celtic Rock (Berthoud)
Classic Blues for Electric Guitar (Sokolow)
Famous Guitar Lines (McCabe)
Famous Guitar Lines Made Easy/Large Print Edition (McCabe)
Mel Bay Guitar University Rock Curriculum: Foundations of Rock:
Guitar Riffs in the Style of the 60's & 70's (Finn)
Mel Bay Guitar University: Rock Guitar Masterclass Vol. 1/60 Tapping Licks (Anastassakis)